T0147177

TO STIR CRAZY
AND BACK

John J. Spadafora

WESTBOW
PRESS®
A DIVISION OF THOMAS NELSON
& ZONDERVAN

WestBow Press books may be ordered through booksellers or by contacting:

WestBow Press
A Division of Thomas Nelson & Zondervan
1663 Liberty Drive
Bloomington, IN 47403
www.westbowpress.com
1 (866) 928-1240

Scripture taken from the King James Version of the Bible.

ISBN: 978-1-9736-7646-1 (sc)
ISBN: 978-1-9736-7647-8 (hc)
ISBN: 978-1-9736-7645-4 (e)

Library of Congress Control Number: 2019915537

Print information available on the last page.

WestBow Press rev. date: 07/31/2020

ACKNOWLEDGMENTS

This book was started at the request of many friends I have met at various parties. Somehow, I began to tell the story to one or two people casually. The next thing I noticed is that I had the attention of everyone. They then implored me to tell the whole story. Needless to say I was elated that it was received with such warmth and laughter.

I finally decided to write the book but after I wrote 3 chapters a family crisis arose, and the book got shelved. Many years went by and my eldest daughter Kelly asked me to finish writing the book. After much persistence she made me sit down every Thursday for 2 hours and complete the book.

I can't thank her enough for her persistence. From then on, many family members have tried to encourage and help make sure it came to fruition. Thank you all for caring.

Contents

Chapter 1

VACATION

This story begins in Florida in the summer of 1974. I had a full-time job as a pharmaceutical salesman while actively investing in real estate. Real estate investments were very profitable, so I was making excellent money. Profits were more than modest and steady. All my efforts were directed toward making money.

Although I had a wonderful wife and two adoring daughters, I ate, slept, and drank making money. As financial goals were set and achieved, I still felt something was missing. The investments started small and gradually became larger. Life's challenge was all about the money, but the eagerness to get there was wearing away. The question "Is it worth it?" seemed to keep popping up.

I kept asking myself, "Is this really what I want to do? Work hard just to make money?" Somehow life didn't seem complete. The money wasn't creating enough satisfaction. While I enjoyed making the money and seemed really happy, my wife felt things really needed to change. She didn't tell me; she just kept things to herself and devised a plan that would change the course of our lives in such a marked way that the battle wounds are still not healed twenty years later.

It started with her innocent request. "Honey, do you think we could take a trip to Pennsylvania?"

I didn't find this question unreasonable. A visit to her relatives in a northern state didn't make me feel threatened. I was grounded in Florida. My father had moved our family from Massachusetts when I was young, and remembering those cold winters made me thankful for my father's decision. To this day, as I recall the beautiful, sunshiny days and the sparkling waters of Florida, I still wonder how I could have been coaxed away from such a tropical paradise. I was truly spoiled. From time to time, our family went north to visit, and my feeling that I was living where I wanted to be was reinforced. I found it hard to understand why people in the North didn't move south to a warmer climate, especially Florida.

My wife couldn't help but notice how distant from her idea of marital bliss and storybook family life I was. But she didn't know how to change me. So only as a woman can, she convinced her man to take a family trip. After six years of marriage, this would be our first vacation. It wouldn't be an extravagant one. It would be an automobile adventure. We played games, we sang, and we had fun. But it wasn't too much fun to stop at almost every other restroom with two small children taking turns asking for a potty stop. Once we reached Pennsylvania, I noticed how green everything was. It was rich and lush and a deep green. Florida, by contrast, was sandy and dry.

We enjoyed our stay with her relatives, and everyone seemed to have a good time. We tried to help them with some small chores and show appreciation for their wonderful hospitality. After we were there for a few days, Gloria, my wife, asked me whether I wanted to see where she had grown up. She wanted to share with me some of the places that had meant so much to her as a child. Again, not suspecting anything, I was game.

She directed me to a city called Somerset, where we found a big field on the outskirts. Her face took on an immediate glow. She asked me to stop the car, and she immediately got the children out. The next thing I knew, all of them were running through the tall grass, giggling, frolicking, and just having a grand time. I joined them. The wind blowing in our faces was unusual because we just never did anything like this in Florida. Don't misunderstand me. Florida was exciting, and there were things to do. But you just didn't go running through a field. You see, there are sandspurs in Florida, and if you ever got one stuck to your skin, you would never think about walking through a field again.

This different outlook had an effect on us, especially my wife. Her secret plan was starting to work. She then commented that we should visit some small towns in the area just to see what they were like. Our first stop was a town called Ligonier. This was truly a town out of a storybook. In the center of town was the square with a gazebo large enough for a good-sized band to perform there; at least I imagined that might be its purpose. The streets and sidewalks that surrounded the gazebo were made of cobblestone. And at every corner of the center of this town, there were stores that just beckoned you to enter them.

The ice cream shop, with its freshly painted pastel colors of ice cream, defied you not to enter it. The Italian restaurant was so small and quaint that you just knew an old couple from Italy had to run it. The town hall probably had the most prominence, yet its scale didn't dwarf the rest of the central area. The butcher, the baker, and the candlestick maker all seemed to be where they should be, placed in a Currier and Ives picture. We got caught up in the excitement. You couldn't just drive through this town; you wanted to be part of it.

We spent most of the day immersed in the town of Ligonier. Finally, Gloria suggested we see more of the countryside. I readily agreed. The outing was exhilarating.

We drove approximately thirty minutes while just admiring the countryside. At least that was what I was doing until my wife said, "Pull over. I want to ask that man something."

I pulled over, and Gloria said, "Excuse me, sir."

He politely acknowledged her and started walking over to the car. Gloria then astonished me. She said, "I understand that there is a farm around here for sale. Could you tell me where it is?"

I looked at her in complete amazement. What could have possessed her even to ask such a question? Yes, we were excited about all these new wonders we were experiencing, but this was only a vacation. We were supposed to enjoy ourselves and then go home. Home was Florida. Home was sunshine. Home was the Gulf of Mexico. Home was the beach. Why had she asked this total stranger whether he knew of a particular farm for sale?

The man said there was a farm for sale down this very road next to his property.

Gloria responded, "Oh, that's great!"

Gloria and I both thanked him, but I didn't know why.

As we drove off according to his instructions, I looked at her and asked how she knew about this farm. She responded, "I think someone mentioned that there was a farm for sale in this area."

I knew we were at least one hour and fifteen minutes from her relatives' home, and I recalled that she had said she was about four years old when they lived in Pennsylvania. We had driven too far for this trip just to be coincidence. We had spent half the day admiring the countryside, or so I thought.

I looked at her with an accusatory look, and she immediately blurted out, "I thought you would like to know what farms are selling for."

She knew I was always a sucker for a good investment, and if I saw something that might be profitable, I would surely get involved in it. All our investing was in real estate. We'd bought many homes, remodeled them, and sold them. We'd built an apartment house and started a day care center, all with the intent of making money.

Gloria reminded me that farmland was real estate, but farming didn't seem to be a good real estate investment to me. Farming was a way of life. A farm is a place other people had where I might like to visit, if I were to have the unlikely urge. It's a place you see on the news where people have a hard time because of a bad crop this year or because the price of beef drops due to a population explosion of baby cows. I had never been around a farm. I had been around land but never a farm.

We didn't go far before we came upon a wide-open area with a farmhouse. The house was a little larger than a typical farmhouse. It had two stories, a large wraparound front porch, and wood lap siding—and it was definitely old. Across the way was a huge barn. It got my attention. It was at least thirty feet by eighty feet and three stories tall, with a silo to the right. It was a typical farm building with cow stalls below, and then in front was a ramp that allowed one to drive up to the second level, which held a large hayloft. It badly needed repairing, but I was still impressed with the size.

This farm was so different from anything I was used to that it started to mesmerize me. Everything looked so beautiful. The grass was green, the trees were green, and the ground had rich, black dirt. It was quite a contrast from the city life of Florida.

We drove up to the house, and an elderly woman came to the door. Gloria cried out, "Is this the farm that is for sale?"

The woman responded, "Why yes, but how did you find it?"

"Oh, we've been looking for quite a while," Gloria responded with a big smile on her face.

At that point, I realized I was a pawn. My wife had control of me. I just hadn't known it until then.

The woman invited us in, and the nostalgia of this home got to us with its high ceilings, large windows, and the big front porch. I could just picture four or five people sitting on this porch. This wasn't a porch I would just look at. This was an inviting porch that compelled me to sit down and sip lemonade with friends. The feeling was overwhelming. The stories I knew had been told on this porch were like going back in time.

We learned that this farm had been built around the turn of the century. The woman let us know that years ago, this farm had been very well known in the area. It consisted of 213 acres to raise cow's providing the milk for the adjoining town. Its history was well known, even though it had changed hands and was no longer active. She further advised us that it "definitely had a historical background."

I saw that most of the field was fenced off. The farm needed a great deal of repair. The silo had no roof. One side of that enormous barn had some missing boards, and I could easily see one place in the roof that needed patching. But other than those two areas, the barn looked pretty secure.

There was also an additional small house. Picture just one eight-by-10 room built like a house, with a pitched roof and a little chimney. The two windows were small but well positioned for the size of the house. The entry door was half glass, so there was just enough light on the inside. The woman explained that the house was where the hired hand had stayed. That detail immediately got my attention.

Then I asked what the round structure was. She explained that when the farm had been in full operation, the milk had been processed and kept there. Now it was used as a place for a saddle, tack, and just plain storage. In the field there were two horses, and by the barn an old red tractor looked like a big toy. It had a crank on the front like one would use on a Model T Ford to start it. The woman was very proud to inform us that the crank was how you started the tractor—there was no key, just a crank.

I soon realized that while being a bit overwhelmed, this city boy was also being sucked in. The ambiance was quickly growing on me. I had seen other farms from a distance but here, up close, was a farm in waiting. I could just imagine how many cows had been there at one time, but now the fields were empty except for a golden palomino and a black-and-white pony. I had seen a lot of Roy Rogers as a kid, so I knew my horses, at least from TV. I enjoyed watching the horses as they grazed on that rich, green grass. You knew they were truly at home—laid back, the epitome of tranquility.

Although the total farm had 213 acres, I could see that only about sixty acres had been cleared, and trees outlined the rest. She explained some of the unusual conditions that made this farm unique. There was a spring that ran from the mountains through the property; it was approximately one-quarter of a mile from the house. The original owners had made a spillway, which fed cold mountain spring water through underground pipes to the house by gravity. Watering troughs for the animals had been set up in the same manner.

After we toured the farm, we went into the house, and the women asked, "Where are you from?"

We explained that we were from Florida and were visiting relatives locally.

Then she asked us, "Why are you looking at this farm?"

I looked at Gloria and waited for her to respond. With a big grin, she said, "I wanted my husband to see what a farm was like in Pennsylvania. As a child, I grew up on a farm not too far away, and I wanted my husband to see one firsthand. We have been married for approximately six years, and this is our very first vacation away from Florida." She further explained that since we were in her state, she wanted me to take it all in, especially because I was a city boy.

The woman said she understood and went onto say, "The farm would be a tremendous investment for anyone who bought it. It's well known in these parts. It's called the Patterson farm." She went on to explain that in its day it had been the attraction of the local village.

We learned that her brother had bought the farm and held onto it as an investment; he had allowed her to live there rent free—I guess to ensure no vandals would decide to move in.

She said, "I have been happy to be here, but now that I'm older, I want to move back into the village. My brother understands." She'd agreed to help him sell the place and then move into town.

She told us about the herds of deer that graze in the pasture. Again, she managed to make my mouth water. I wasn't a hunter, and I didn't even own a gun, but I'd fantasized many times about what it might be like to go hunting. Now she was making me melt before I even knew what was happening.

We spoke with her for about an hour and a half, and then she invited us to stay for dinner. We politely declined and left. The entire trip back to Gloria's relatives was filled with chatter about the farm. The peaceful, serene, and scenic landscape was just the opposite of the hustle in Florida. As we rode along, I realized this was the antithesis of the demanding, structured life I'd lived back home.

When we got back to the home of Gloria's relatives, her Aunt Rose asked, "Where did you go today?"

Gloria said, "We went for a ride in the country."

I quickly added, "Yeah, Gloria wanted to show me a farm somewhere near Ligonier."

Aunt Rose's eyes lit up. "Ligonier was well thought of in the area." She further explained that it was revered by most who visited. By way of history, she said the Mellon family, founders of the Mellon Bank & Gulf Oil Company, were somehow linked to Ligonier.

That evening, as we prepared for bed, Gloria looked at me with the biggest smile. "What do you think of Pennsylvania?"

I had to admit it was definitely different. Its beauty and seemingly slow, laid-back pace had really captivated me.

It was hard to sleep that night. Although the farm wouldn't be considered one of my normal real estate investments, I felt it had a lot going for it.

The purchase price was $69,000. In today's economy, that doesn't sound like much, but in 1974, one could purchase a very nice home in an attractive neighborhood on a one-third-of-an-acre lot for $38,000.

In comparison, here was this beautiful rolling land with a large farmhouse, a gigantic barn, a house for the hired help, and a round tack shop. A golden Palomino, a pony, a tractor, and 213 acres—all this for only $69,000. This truly got my attention which caused my mind to race all night.

Gloria had planted a seed, which I couldn't stop from growing. No plans were set for the following day, so I asked Gloria whether she would like to go back to Ligonier and possibly visit the farm again. She smiled her best smile. She knew her plan was working.

After arriving in Ligonier, I remembered that Gloria had written down the farm owner's telephone number. I asked her to give it to me while we were eating at that quaint Italian restaurant. I said, "I'd like to call him and to talk to him a little." The fact that the farm was in the middle of nowhere and had no active city excitement around it became my Achilles' heel. Before I called the owner, I called his sister and asked to see the farm one more time. She readily agreed.

Once we were there, it seemed to look more beautiful than it had before. It was hard to believe, but this farm was growing on me. I told the woman I was going to call her brother and set up an appointment to meet with him. She said, "He lives in the village of Bolivar which is approximately four miles from here." She then said she would call him for me. I agreed, and she informed me that he would be available in about half an hour. She then gave us directions, and we were on our way.

We drove slowly through the village of Bolivar to get an idea of what it was like. The first thing we noticed was a sign that read "Population 462." In Florida there must have been

462 people living on our development alone. As we continued through this village, we noticed only one very small grocery store. The sign on the only gas station indicated that it doubled as a repair shop. Then I noticed something that seemed out of place: two one-way streets.

As we drove around the block, following the one-way street, we came to the home of Mr. Hawks. The outside didn't look like he was well to do; however, once we were inside, we could tell this man had an appreciation for the finer things in life. The furniture was ornate, and many fine articles were being displayed. This man surely was in a very comfortable financial position.

We let him know that his property intrigued us and that we wanted to learn more about it. We started asking questions, such as how long he had owned it, why he was selling it, and finally how much money it would take to purchase it. He began telling us that he had never bought it as an investment but rather because of its history. He went on to say that he had never lived there but that at one time it had been the center of activity in the area. A politician had owned it, and that was how it had gotten the name of the Patterson farm. I began to realize he was trying to build up the value of the farm, but since I didn't know the Patterson's, this detail meant nothing to me.

He said, "I could probably take a little less." I then tried to find out how much less, but he wanted me to give him an offer. Then I told him I really wasn't serious about buying it. I was just interested in how such a property was valued. Then I found myself mentioning all the flaws associated with the farm I had noticed. You would almost think I was interested. I began to scare myself.

Then he brought me to my senses by saying that the history

of the farm offset any flaws that might be present. I told him that we appreciated his time, said good-bye, and drove off. We went back to Gloria's relatives, finished our stay, and finally returned to Florida.

I was the top salesman in the southeast division within my company. I had a company car and an expense account, and my bonus almost matched my salary. I'd built a new apartment house the year before, and it was fully rented. I'd started a day care for children that was doing very well.

We lived in a very nice house in a prestigious neighborhood. We were making money. Life was good, as if making money was the only criteria for having a good life. Well, it's not. The trip had made me realize that fact. I was sacrificing precious time away from my family. I had been introduced to a whole other world, a seemingly peaceful world, a world that made me slowdown in spite of myself.

Imagine 213 acres and a large five-bedroom house with a living room, a dining room, a huge kitchen, and a very large room that didn't have a name. I'm sure that when the farm had been in full service, this was the room that kept the boots, farm work clothes, and probably a place to relax if you didn't want to mess up the house.

The seed had been planted. It had been generously watered. And it was definitely growing.

After our vacation, when something didn't go right, I remembered that serene setting at the farm. But I had to keep plugging, for I was a go-getter at making money. It seemed like an opportune time to sell the apartment complex, so I did. This sale created a financial windfall.

However, my sales position with the pharmaceutical

company was about to change. The bonus structure was going to be revamped, and I, who made one of the largest bonuses, was going to have my bonus cut by approximately two-thirds. How could they do this to me? I'd developed a cocky attitude, which I would later regret. I was now making more money than I had a right to; even with the change, I had no right to complain.

My boss realized I was going to be affected greatly and tried to appease me with the promise that I could have his job when he retired in a couple of years. But I didn't want his job, since he was always in a plane flying off somewhere. I already felt guilty enough about leaving my children too much.

Although we rarely spoke about the farm, Gloria felt that the time was right to bring in the harvest. The seed was now fully grown; it was ripe and ready for the picking. She saw that I was letting problems get way out of proportion and said, "Have you thought any more about the Patterson farm?"

I didn't want to admit it, but I had. I told her I had thought about the farm, but it was out of the question. I made my money in the city; besides, what would I do in the country? She reminded me that we now had a pretty good nest egg saved and that I always seemed to do well at everything I did. Her timing was impeccable.

She said, "Why don't you offer him a crazy number and see what he says?"

"No." Then I thought, *If I got it for a steal, it would be a great investment.* I finally agreed to offer $55,000.

I guessed he wouldn't take the offer, and that would be the end of the matter. In a moment of weakness, I called him, and we had a casual conversation. Finally, he asked if I wanted to buy the farm, to which I answered, "I'd like to offer you fifty-five thousand."

He immediately said, "No, I couldn't possibly sell it for that!"

I told him I also thought it was worth more and that I totally understood his decision. When we got off the phone, I thought, *Good*. The farm was now out of my system. It wasn't a steal, so there was no need to even think about it anymore.

Over the next two weeks, I began to settle down and accept the changes my company had made. I started looking for my next conquest and the potential challenges that lay ahead. I started looking at an interest in an available marina. Two weeks later, out of the blue, I got a call from Mr. Hawks.

He said, "I've decided to accept your offer."

My mind began racing. *What have I done?* Realizing that I was about to make a serious decision, I said, "Mr. Hawks, before I agree to this, I need to come up and look it over one more time."

He said that would be all right and that we could stay at the farm rather than go to a hotel. He further said, "My sister would be happy to cook for you." He certainly was being very generous.

We had first visited Pennsylvania in the summer, and it was now midwinter. Gloria said, "We have to get some heavy clothes."

We began to get excited about the possibilities. My mother-in-law cared for the children, and we flew into Pittsburgh, rented a car, and drove to the farm. It was now 32 degrees. With our coming from Florida's 80 degrees, the temperature was a big shock, but with all the excitement, the weather contrast seemed acceptable. As we arrived at the farm, it started snowing large, glistening flakes that gently landed everywhere. Beautiful didn't even come close to describing this winter wonderland.

Our minds were made up, and we finalized the arrangements to buy the farm within the first two hours of our arrival.

Chapter 2

MOVE TO THE FARM

After our trip to seal the deal, it was time for us to orchestrate the move from the sunny South to the cold wilderness of Pennsylvania. The difficult part was telling our children.

This was going to be a very different life than what they could ever imagine at their ages. Florida was where they'd been born. It was where their cousins, grandparents, aunts, uncles, and friends lived, and it was the only home they knew.

After telling the children, Kerry, our youngest, seemed to go with the flow as always. No matter what the news, Kerry was always as happy-go-lucky as could be.

Her personality matched her Shirley Temple curly brown hair, which was always bouncing. She was exuberant and full of life, an entrepreneur at heart. She was always game for anything that presented itself as an adventure.

For example, one day after we arrived at the farm, I told both girls, "Whoever kills the most flies today gets a penny for each dead fly". At the age of four, her young mind altered the thought I'd envisioned. I came home to find a mound of dead dried flies on a paper towel. Kerry was looking at me as if she knew she'd won the big catch of the day and also knew Daddy would be proud. I knew we had quite a few flies, but a whole army was now sitting on the table, ready to be tallied for the winnings of the day. What she'd actually done was scoop up all the dead flies from the windowsills throughout the house. I had to hand it to her. I hadn't really specified how the flies were to be captured. Now all the windowsills were clean. It was the only debt I ever paid while laughing at the same time.

My daughter Kelly, on the other hand, was quite a different story. After telling her we were moving, I might as well have turned the water hose on full blast. A gusher of teary-eyed emotion poured out of her blue eyes. She wasn't as open to change as her sister and didn't bounce back as easily. I could tell she was analyzing the situation with every question her young mind could fathom. Moving means you leave. Leaving means grandparents don't come with you. Leaving means no more Uncle Ray to wrestle with or Aunt Sandy to make you laugh. Leaving means no cousins to play with. Leaving means everything you hold dear is now being torn away forever. At least, this was what she verbalized. Her only consolation was that she would be allowed to ride with Daddy in the moving truck. When she heard that promise, I became a hero, and all was right with the world.

When moving day finally came, Gloria drove one car with our youngest daughter, Kerry; Babette, our Poodle, and our cat, Boofull. Boofull is what you get when you tell a two-year-old to say *beautiful*. It comes out as *Boofull*. I secured the biggest Ryder truck, which pulled the biggest U-Haul trailer available Kelly, our oldest daughter, and our Siberian husky Tasha, rode with me in the huge Ryder Truck.

We tried to make our stops as efficient as possible, but for some reason, the fuel stops, potty stops, pit stops for animals, and meal stops didn't coincide. We managed to make a two-day trip last just short of one week.

I was so wrapped up in my blissful thoughts of our new home-to-be that I never checked with Gloria regarding how the trip was affecting her. However, she made it her priority to inform me when we stopped to eat. We sat down, and she blurted out, "U-Haul rents trucks, U-Haul rents trailers, U-Haul rents trucks that pull trailers, U-Haul rents blankets, U-Haul rents dollies, and U-Haul sells boxes to put in trucks!" I thought this speech was strange until I looked out the window at our trailer, the trailer she had been following for the past six days. I then burst out laughing, realizing that the words she'd recited were written on the back door of the trailer she had been staring at for almost a week.

Soon we began to see hills, which later turned into mountains. This change in terrain became quite a strain on the truck, and parking this rig was a feat in itself. Finally, after wondering whether we would ever get there, we arrived at the farm. It was near the end of the sixth day.

"We made it!" we all shouted in unison.

We walked through the front door after bodily pushing on it twice. It didn't look quite like the farmhouse we had previously visited, because all the furniture and nice distinctive pictures on the walls were gone. The place actually seemed a bit frightening. As we went from room to room, what we saw was the complete opposite of the complimenting enhancements that had initially graced each room. What we now observed was an old run-down farmhouse.

The floors were bare. The beautiful antique light fixtures that had hung from the ceilings were gone, and in their place were wires hanging from the ceilings with solitary light bulbs. As we entered the bedroom, something was stranger still, but I couldn't at first figure out what was different.

Finally, it dawned on us. "Aha!" I said. "No closets."

We tried to think back to the time when we stayed there. Gloria explained that she remembered the pretty armoire we hung our clothes in. We'd never realized it was the only place to hang clothes. When we got to the kitchen, it looked like a bomb had exploded. Not only were there no appliances, but there were no cabinets or lights; even the linoleum that had once covered the floor had been removed. All that was left was a solitary empty cabinet holding the sink. *Everything* but the kitchen sink had been removed.

I walked outside to the front porch steps and sat there in disbelief. "What have I done?" I murmured to myself. "It will take a lifetime to make this house a home." This wasn't the laid-back life I'd envisioned. *Yes, I've done it. I left my fast, profitable lifestyle to go to a nightmare? And to think, I did this on purpose. I paid good money for this event to take place. How was I actually looking forward to this? I must be an idiot. It's finally setting in. I have made one of the biggest mistakes of my life.*

Little did I know how true those thoughts would become. I hadn't said an audible word while sitting on the steps during this time of mental self-flagellation. But my face must have reflected my thoughts, because at this point Gloria grabbed the children and held them protectively close, as if to remind me that she was the mother of two helpless little girls who needed her love to survive—just in case I had connected the dots and realized it was she who had planned, schemed, and set this well-laid-out plan. Now, after coming to fruition, it brought only disappointment and disbelief.

I, John Spadafora, had been suckered into the craziest nightmare which I hoped was all a bad dream. However, I was awake, and it wasn't getting any better.

After being forced to accept the obvious, we decided not to spend the night at the farm. Instead, we drove to the quaint town of Ligonier and spent a restless night at a motel.

The next day we went back to the farm and reassessed our situation. The mental list I had rehearsed all through the night verified the following:

1) I quit a very desirable, lucrative job.
2) I gave up my ability to invest in an area I was familiar with.
3) I gave up being respected as a successful businessman in the community.
4) I sold my beautiful home across from the Gulf of Mexico.
5) I bought a farmhouse that should have been leveled instead of turning it into my worst nightmare.

After my assessment, it was pretty clear we were going to have to stay. I just couldn't spend another week on the road. *Will we have to stay in this house in these conditions?* I questioned. It would be tough, but we could do it. *I'm a survivor!* At least that is what I was trying to convince myself of.

It was time to unload the truck. We are in the middle of nowhere. Where in the blue blazes was I going to find help? Just about then, my neighbor came and introduced himself.

"Hey, I'm your neighbor, Andy. Are you moving in?" he said.

"Yes sir, I was about to," I answered.

He then asked, "Do ye need help?" This was the first uplifting moment of this whole disheartening predicament.

My heart leaped. "Oh, would you?" I said.

"Why sure!" he said.

I couldn't believe it. I was so thankful. I was actually getting help to move into this nightmare. If I had only come to my senses, I would have said, "Yes, help me turn this truck around and point me south."

Andy helped back up the truck to the front stairs. Because of the size of the truck, the ramp got us only as close as the bottom step. While unloading, I walked backward up the porch stairs, holding one end of the furniture. Andy's position was holding the other end while walking forward. The furniture was heavy and awkward, but we were managing. First one step, then another, and then a third.

I was about to go to the fourth step when the wood gave way under me. I was scared and stunned as both of my feet hit the ground. I was surprised that I didn't get hurt. Then almost at once I started to yell and flail my hands while trying to get out of the stairs.

My family and new neighbor stared at me in disbelief. They couldn't help but wonder what was going on. I must have been a sight, because under the steps was a heavily populated hornets' nest, and I had just shot my bottom half through their home. Instantly I felt something stinging me and then another. I must have bolted faster than ever before, because everyone began laughing.

When we finally finished unloading the truck, there were boxes piled everywhere. For some strange reason, the act of returning the truck and trailer brought some sort of relief. I'm not sure whether it was because of the arduous hours on the road or the torture of unloading the truck, but the act of returning it meant that the decision to return to Florida had been put to rest. Whatever the reason, I now had a better outlook on the future.

After we set up the beds, we made pathways through the house while moving boxes around to create a maze. We sat down to collect our thoughts. We badly needed appliances, something to hang our clothes on, cabinets for the kitchen, and light fixtures.

That afternoon we returned to Ligonier for a well-deserved meal at the little Italian restaurant, after which we took a ride to a larger town in Pennsylvania, Latrobe. I was impressed to find that Latrobe was the home of the famous golfer Arnold Palmer. We purchased our appliances and groceries, then returned to our new home.

The next day, it was difficult to find something to keep the girls occupied because of the monumental task that lay before us. Kelly and Kerry were only five and four years old respectively. It was now time to commission my little fly slayers to resume the hunt for flies, dead or alive. Because of the age of the old farmhouse, you could almost slip your little pinky through the cracks in the windows and doors. This was a welcome sign for any fly to enter. The going price again was a penny apiece. They had done such a good job that by days end, I had to write an IOU. The next day I caught Kerry picking out some of the dead flies from the trash and recycling them for profit. To this day, when I see Kerry, I look for my wallet.

While calculating the needs and costs to make the repairs to the house, I noticed that the electrical hadn't been updated since knob tube wiring was introduced. The bathroom hadn't been modernized. After the long day, we were very tired, and all went to sleep early.

The next morning, I went into the bathroom, and in the corner, there was an old-timey cast-iron corner sink with individual hot and cold porcelain handles. I turned on the cold-water faucet, and very cold spring-fed water came out of the faucet. So, I turned on the hot water handle. After putting a plug in the bottom of the sink to hold the water, the hot water instantly flowed, filling the sink ready for me to shave.

Oh! Wonder of wonders! Halfway through shaving, I thought I should clean off my blade with more hot water. But when I turned the handle, it came off in my hand, and hot water went spewing up to the ceiling. I panicked and yelled, "Gloria!" as if she could do something about it. I ran out of the bathroom and down to the hot water tank in the basement to shut off the feed line. I had learned earlier that shutting off the electric was necessary to prevent harming the heating elements. I located a fuse box next to the coal bin, something I had neglected to acquaint myself with before the delusion of the wonderful farm life.

In the kitchen, Gloria and the children were wondering what I would utter in my frustration. I said nothing. I knew it wasn't their fault, even though I really wanted to vent. This supposedly peaceful life was now one of survival. I could never have foreseen what was to unfold in reality. I knew now, on top of everything else, that I was in need of a plumber.

As I began my search for one, I soon found that there was only one plumber for the population of 462 people. Of course, he was very busy; he had no competition. While speaking to him about the problem, he assured me that he would come promptly in two or three days.

We forgot about going to town and focused our attention on unpacking and putting things away. We could foresee this mountain of boxes being brought down to a little hill. We worked hard, and the project was taking shape. Despite the wet morning's events, the day had actually resulted in becoming a fruitful one. The range and refrigerator were delivered. So other than the hot water faucet being broken, the day turned into one of accomplishments.

By day's end, we all needed baths. Gloria put the stopper in the bottom of the tub to hold the water and boiled water to pour into the tub. We surely couldn't bathe the kids in cold mountain spring water. My kids really looked cute in that big, old fashioned tub. I was tired and mellowed after a long, eventful day, and was now taking note of the little things that brought a smile to my face. For the moment life seemed good.

After the kids were finished, Gloria proceeded to empty the bath water down the tub drain by pulling the stopper out of the drain hole. However, the water wouldn't go down the drain. For some unknown reason, there were six of the old porcelain white cross handles in the wall. One was used to get cold water in the tub. But the others left us wondering what they were for. She tried turning them all, but nothing happened. I got a coat hanger and tried to put it through the drain to unplug it but to no avail.

I went into the basement and dismembered the plumbing under the tub, but no water came out. I didn't understand. I used the coat hanger and tried to push it up through the bottom of the tub drain. I kept jamming it up, but nothing happened. At the same time, in her frustration Gloria was "trying to help," and she started turning all the knobs in any direction they would go.

I stopped and pointed a bright flashlight up to the drain to observe what obstruction was causing the problem. And then it happened. The dirty tub water came pouring out all over my face and body. Gloria hollered, "I found the problem! It was one of the handles that controls the drain. It's working now!"

I slowly walked up the stairs. When she saw me drenched in dirty tub water, she turned and ran for the kids. Although I never struck my wife, I think her feelings of guilt from her perceived plot made her worthy of a major altercation.

I never said a word. After Gloria realized I was too tired to say anything, she assured me that I'd feel better after a nice, warm bath. She told me to go upstairs and get some nightclothes while she prepared the bath water. At this point, anything was good news compared to the current situation. With a half-hearted smile, I went upstairs and got out of the wet clothes. I put my robe on and brought my dry nightclothes to the bathroom with me. The tub was now full of water.

With one hand on one side of this high tub and the other on the opposite side, I proceeded to steady myself as I slid in. As I slowly made my descent, the frigid water was so cold that I lost my grip on the sides and became completely immersed. Since Gloria was standing there, she noticed as I bobbed up out of the water that I gasped for air and that my skin color was a little blue. It was then that she realized she had forgotten to boil the water for my bath. I instantaneously made a loud "Ahhhhhhhhhhhhhh!"

I couldn't get out fast enough. I was gasping for breath during my retreat. The last thing I remember, Gloria was running to the children's room again.

Getting settled in the house took about one week. We were now evaluating our priorities for what our next steps should be.

The farmhouse was old and in much need of repair. The logical step now was to go ahead and make the repairs. We would then be able to give the place our personal touch to make it our new home. With that idea in mind, it was time to visit the local village of Bolivar.

After the first week, with all its ups and downs, which seemed to be more downs than ups, we settled in. The commotion of initial events was behind us, and we were actually able to relax. In relaxing I finally noticed the farm often seemed a bit mysterious.

There was something we hadn't noticed before or were accustom to. It was the sound of silence. Coming from the city, I was used to hearing neighbors talking, an occasional ambulance, motorcycles and cars driving by. I had adjusted to sleeping with these sounds. But this silence was nerve racking.

Then we started hearing new sounds we had never heard before. It was a night owl. I had heard it on TV and kidded about the sounds I assume owls would make, but this was real, and it was just outside. We started to hear other sounds. We started to fantasize about the possibilities of raccoons and possums. But this was too loud. And we heard one sound after another. It sounded like a loud snort that repeated again and again. My thoughts raced fearing wild boars were waiting outside the door

I was now panicking. Was it a bear, a bob cat or an unknown intruder? Whatever it was, it was close to the house.

Dressed only in my boxer shorts, I quickly grabbed a 1929 pistol Gloria had inherited from her grandfather and slowly walked down the stairs. Holding the pistol slightly up in the air, like I'd seen on TV, I started having second thoughts about firing the old relic. I had never fired it before. What if it backfired, misfired, or blew up? I knew this response was possible because I had also seen that scenario play out on TV. I then heard some sort of animal sounds again, but they were a little louder this time. At that point, I forgot about the gun. I turned on the front porch lights, walked to the end of the porch, and looked into pure darkness. Whatever was making these disturbing sounds was nowhere to be seen.

The next day I scouted around the area and found some deer droppings, and I reasoned that a deer must have been the creature making the noise.

While looking around outside, I noticed the exterior entrance to the basement. As I went down to investigate, I realized it wasn't locked after bodily pushing on it. I then came face-to-face with our heating source, an old coal furnace. I figured that eventually we would rid ourselves of the old relic in hopes of installing a more modern heating system. However, I would have to learn to stoke a coal furnace until then. I thought I really had gotten pretty good at it, but the fire never lasted until morning. First thing in the morning when I woke up, my feet hit the cold floor, and I shivered until I could bundle up to go to the basement and restart the furnace.

Chapter 3

INTRODUCTION TO THE VILLAGE

W e finally came to a day that lacked any pressing issues. Gloria thought it would be a great time to visit Bolivar. We had briefly visited Bolivar while on our vacation adventure. The first stop was the "Apothecary", an old-timey drugstore. I felt it was important to get a first aid kit. I foresaw some manual labor, work unfamiliar to me. Surely the potential of hard work could produce a minor cut here and there. For me, anything I did that didn't produce money was hard work. When we walked through the door of the Apothecary, we were taken back in time. It was just like watching an old movie. On the left was an awesome marble soda fountain with a lever to be pulled down to get whatever flavor soda was desired. The ceiling was unusually high. The shelves were filled with a large variety of medications for such a small town.

We had never seen anything like this museum of a place. It was early 1900s. The mirrors behind the counter were identical to those of old western saloons I had seen in movies. The soda fountain had barstools that spun around.

The girls dashed up to the soda fountain, climbed on

the stools, looked at me, and said, "Daddy, can we have a milkshake?"

"Of course," I replied.

I noticed that only one employee was working in the store, and we were the only patrons.

Gloria sat with the girls as they drank their milkshakes. Meanwhile, I walked around and looked at the various home remedies I had never heard of or seen before.

I walked to the back of the store, expecting to find a pharmacist. Suddenly the young lady who had served the girls their milkshakes hollered at me from the counter, "We don't have a pharmacist."

I then moseyed back to the front, and she explained, "There is one doctor in town, but he is here only one day a week. If you need a prescription filled, you can go to the next town."

I said, "We are new to the village. Could you tell me what other shops are in town?"

She said, "There is a grocery store right up the road, on the same side of this street. Across the street is a shoe store, and around the corner is a hardware store. Further down the road a way is a butcher on the right." She explained that they were very fortunate to have their own post office in town and that the mayor was also the fire chief. I thanked her for all this information, and we left, having made a new friend.

The first stop was the grocery store. It couldn't have been more than eighteen feet wide and sixty feet deep. The high ceilings were about ten feet tall. The shelves in the store went all the way to the ceiling. In the corner there was a ladder on wheels, which rolled on a track to offer access to the upper shelves. As we looked around, a little, old Italian man greeted us. He had a smile on his face as he asked, "Cana I helpa yu?"

I smiled and said, "We have come to shop." I asked out of curiosity, "How do you get the food off of the top shelves?"

He looked at me as if I were from another planet. He then showed me a long stick with a grapple at one end and a gripper at the other; at the same time he pointed at the rolling ladder.

I looked in astonishment and said, "Cool!"

As we started to shop, he followed us around. "Ara yu visitin' soma one here?" he asked.

"We just moved here," I replied.

He immediately stopped, then leaned back with a surprised look on his face. His expression was now one of concern, almost as if this was a town you move away from but not into. He then spoke up. "Whera yu mova?"

"We bought a farm," I answered.

"Wata farm?"

"The Patterson farm." I retorted. Wondering if he knew of it.

His eyes widened, and with a smirk he asked, "How mucha yu pay?"

I couldn't believe he would ask such an intrusive question. That was too personal for me. So, I said, "I paid enough."

He narrowed his brow and without blinking said, "You pay eh fifty-fife thousand a dollars!"

I couldn't believe my ears. How did he know?

I kept my cool and continued to look around. His next question floored me.

"Where yu getta da monay?"

The audacity of this man! Now, I was irritated and replied, "I worked for it."

"I work eh all of eh my life! I *never* make eh fifty-five thousand eh dollars!"

I looked at him with my cocky attitude and said, "I worked hard."

With that, he stopped. I could see the little wheels turning in his head. Now he must have assumed I was rich. He asked my name, and I then introduced myself and my family.

Immediately, he recognized the name Spadafora to be Italian. And it was then that we became *Pisanos for* life. He then took me to his little garden outside the store and said, "I'ma gonna giva yu some of my hota peppers. I grew thema myself." I could tell how proud he was of his peppers.

My father loved hot peppers, but I trembled at the sight of them. My father assumed I would have this same love for those peppers. As a kid, not knowing any better, when I ate them, my rectum was on fire for the next three days. However, I wasn't about to insult my new Italian friend. I took them with a smile and thanked him, and we were on our way.

Our next stop was the hardware store, and the name was "Hardware Store." The front window of large glass panes made it easy to see inside. The peculiar thing about the hardware store was the unusual manner of payment for purchases. There was no counter or cash register, only a small room divided by glass windows from the waist up and a wall from my waist down. In this see-through room, a lady sat and watched customers as they shopped. When one finished shopping, they brought the items to be purchased up to the glass window. Again, we were the only ones in the store.

We brought all the items to the lady behind the glass. Our purchases were a ladder, paint brushes, caulking, paint, and whatever else we needed to do that was required for our home modernization. The bill came to $99.57. I still had some crisp one-hundred-dollar bills left from our move from Florida, and

I nonchalantly handed her one of the remaining bills. She gave me the change and obviously noticed, by the look on her face, that I had many more such bills in my wallet.

Gloria took the girls to the car, and I brought out the ladder. When I came back, she didn't notice all the things I had left behind under the window on the floor. I bent down to pick up the rest of the supplies. It was then that I heard the lady behind the glass window say, "They paid with a crisp, new one-hundred-dollar bill, and they had others. I don't know if it's all right."

When I stood up, I noticed she was holding the hundred-dollar bill toward the light. When she saw me stand up, she immediately hung up the phone and put down the bill. She asked, "Is there anything else I can help you with?"

"I was just gathering the rest of my purchases. But, um, do you know of any place in town to eat?"

She said, "On your way home on the left side of the road, there is a beige two-story house with no sign, but you will know it because of the cars all around it."

After I got into the car, I told Gloria about the comical encounter I had just experienced. We figured the woman in the store had thought the bill was counterfeit.

We located the beige two-story house just as described with parked cars all around it. We went inside, and much to our surprise, it was a full-fledged bar and restaurant. The woman behind the counter told us to have a seat and said she would be with us in a minute. We sat down and looked around. Based on the other customers' bright-orange attire and camo wear, it was obvious that the bar was full of hunters.

When the lady came to our table, she said, "Hello, I am Annie Potts. This is Annie Potts Restaurant."

Without question it was the first genuine smile of acceptance we had received since we had gotten to the town. We explained that we had just moved to town and bought the Patterson farm.

She immediately had a big smile and a gleam in her eye. "Welcome to Bolivar!"

She put her pad in her apron pocket, sat down with us, and asked where we had come from and why we had moved. We told her we were from Florida and wanted a slower pace of life.

She said, "I want you to know that anything you want is on me." She handed us a menu and said she would be right back. She returned, took our orders, prepared our food, and then came back and sat with us. She began talking with us as if we were family. Her kindness was so sincere; it made us feel that someone was actually happy we were new arrivals.

The next day we painted the kitchen and felt better since the brighter colors seemed to cheer us up. While we were painting, there was a knock at the front door.

Andy, the neighbor who had helped us move in, came by with his father. Andy asked whether his father could hunt groundhogs on our land. He explained that they were good to eat.

All I knew about groundhogs was the annual prediction of future weather from Punxsutawney Phil's shadow every year.

I told them they could hunt all they wanted and could keep all they got.

"Oh no, we would be glad to share them fifty-fifty." I wasn't about to eat anything that couldn't be seen packaged by a butcher under clear cellophane with white Styrofoam under it and a label with an expiration date.

The next day Andy's father came by and offered me some of his fresh-cooked groundhog.

Oh no! I thought. *I can't do this! I can't eat this ... wild animal.* He had the biggest smile on his face, a smile of pride in his tasty, prepared dish. There was no way I could offend him. I reached out and picked up a piece. With everything in me, I took a small bite with great trepidation.

He said, "Oh, dig in! Get you a *big* bite."

I took a bigger bite, closed my eyes, and started to chew. Much to my surprise, the groundhog was very delicious. I opened my eyes and said, "That's really good!"

He looked at me and emphatically exclaimed, "Of course that's good." His chest seemed to swell with pride. I tasted my first wildlife, and I really enjoyed it.

He invited me to come by his house the next day and said they were gathering hay to put in a loft. I thought it would be neighborly to go, so I consented.

The next day I asked Gloria whether she wanted to come with me to visit our neighbor. She declined, so I decided to take Kelly with me. We traveled just a couple of miles before we came to their farm. I drove up into the backyard and saw Andy, along with his father and his brother Bill, throwing hay into the loft. As Kelly and I walked toward them, a big, white, beautiful goose suddenly leaned forward and came after us as if we were its next meal.

I heard Andy yell, "Run! His bite is worse than a dog!"

I grabbed Kelly's hand and ran toward our car but realized we weren't going to make it. I picked Kelly up and started running left toward the back porch of their house. Thankfully the steps were steep and high enough to get away from the goose. When we made it to the top, I saw that the goose wasn't following us any longer. It was only looking at us with disgust and squawking loudly.

Andy, his brother Bill, and his father were laughing at the whole fiasco. They were laughing so hard they were crying.

Andy hollered, "I see you've met Jasper!"

I didn't think the situation was a bit funny. Here I was, running for my life with my daughter screaming in my arms, and they were laughing at me? They saw the expression on my face and easily recognized I was very upset. After we all calmed down, we went inside and talked for a while. Before we left Andy's mother gave us a dish of brownies to take home. I was very touched by their hospitality. They were kind, sincere, and hardworking people.

Once at home, we devoured the brownies. They were unbelievably delicious.

The next day, Kerry, our youngest daughter, and I went back to return the brownie dish. This time we went to the front door of the house in hopes of not reliving another encounter with Jasper.

I knocked on the screen door and could see Bill sitting inside. It was an old farmhouse with a very dark living room. Bill told me to come in, so we walked in and sat next to him. I looked around, wondering why it was so dark. As I scanned the room, I noticed what looked like a Beretta handgun between me and Bill. I immediately looked at him and saw him gazing at the ceiling. Just then he reached over, grabbed the gun, and shot at the ceiling, scaring me out of my skin.

Overjoyed, he shouted, "Got him."

I looked up at the ceiling and realized he had shot a BB pistol at a fly. It was now embedded in the acoustical ceiling, which was full of black specks. It then occurred to me that the black specks were prier fly executions. I immediately excused myself, grabbed Kerry, and went home as fast as I could. I told

Gloria about the incident and said our neighbor was crazy and that we must be too for having moved into this place of never-ending surprises and calamities.

Although we couldn't see his trailer from our house, Andy and his wife, Tuttie, lived at the beginning of the dirt road leading to our farm. He was the man who had helped us move into our farm, a most unusual character. He was most easily described as a mountain man. He was large in stature with a heart to match. He worked at the only factory within twenty miles of our house. His job consisted of making wooden pallets.

I had never really heard a mountain man speak before. Andy had a mountain drawl. He pronounced my name as "Jawn." Instead of John. Then he asked questions, such as, "Why did you come here?" I honestly couldn't answer him.

Then he asked, "Jawn, what are you going to do?" Again, he stumped me. To Andy, I must have seemed pretty stupid. To be honest with you, I would have to agree. Andy pictured me as a city slicker and looked at me as if I were a fish out of water.

After finishing our painting project, we went back to town to the post office. We went to register for mail, only to find out there was no home delivery. We would have to go to town to get our mail. While at the post office, I met the mayor of Bolivar, who was also the fire chief. He noticed we were new in the town of Bolivar. He offered any assistance I needed. He proudly pointed out that the town had two one-way streets and only one stop sign with a couple of yield signs. After our conversation, we went to visit the sister of the previous owner of the farm. She'd moved from the farm to one of her brother's houses in town. She was happy to have started living a more active life again. She was our oldest friend in the village and was as delighted to see us as we were to see her.

Gloria walked to the butcher, while I took the car to be serviced. The gas station owner seemed friendly. As we talked, he realized we were the ones who had bought the infamous Patterson farm with its many pastures. He offered me one-third of all the hay if I would allow him to cut it. *Wow, what an offer,* I thought. He was going to cut my grass and not charge me. I was excited and immediately agreed. He also volunteered to put the hay in the barn.

He said, "If you agree, I would like to cut it the next week, and I'll put your portion in the barn."

Of course, I was excited. What a gift! I could just picture the fields being cut and well groomed. I asked him whether he had ever seen rattlesnakes.

He said, "Sure, I always carry a pistol with me in the fields."

I'd never given any thought to poisonous snakes and wondered why that thought had never crossed my mind before. Now I couldn't get it out of my mind. The owner of the gas station shared some of the idiosyncrasies of the town as our conversation went on.

The most surprising revelation was that one person performed three major occupations. There was one undertaker in town—not that this was unusual, but what was unusual was that he advertised specials. It was an incentive to get me to die and have him bury me, I assumed. However, this was a man of many hats and titles. He was also the mayor and fire chief. What an entrepreneur. For some reason, this news didn't go well with me.

I had another unusual neighbor. His name was Walter, and he was in his late thirties. He had a full-grown beard. When he spoke, I became mesmerized by looking for his lips to open in the middle of all that hair. One day after he had argued with his wife, his father-in-law went to his house. So, he went out to greet him with his pistol in his back pocket. I asked him whether he would have used it against his father-in-law.

He said, "You got that right!"

I asked him why his father-in-law had come by.

He said, "Beats me, but he sure wasn't going to take my wife away!"

I was now revaluating my life. I had been a citizen of Bolivar for only three weeks, yet I felt as if I had left the continent. Why had I abandoned that wonderful, predictable, hurried, crazy city life? Oh yeah, life was about to slow down. My outlook on *everything* was changing drastically and coming to what seemed like it might be a dead end.

This was so different from the fast pace of Florida, a life I was used to. It was quaint. Not only was life slow, but we had definitely gone back in time—not only in the buildings but in attitudes as well. It was a puzzling feeling but one I somehow wanted to experience. I was looking forward to what would come next.

Chapter 4

BATS IN THE BELFRY

We had just started to settle in after about three weeks. The summer days had been great to appreciate what our farm had to offer. It was finally taking shape after all the repair work we did. Then the first rain came. It was calming to hear the rain tapping on the roof while I was lying in bed.

Suddenly, we heard something rustling in the attic. *Possibly a rodent*, I thought. After about an hour, an unusual smell began to develop. I couldn't figure out where the odor was coming from. I knew neither Gloria nor myself had released any stinky methane gas.

I turned on the light, got a flashlight, and pointed it at a small door; about thirty inches tall, at the end of the bedroom. I opened the door. The area was too short to be a closet. It must have been meant for storage. I peered into the storage space; about ten feet away there seemed to be a mound. I couldn't make out what it was but reasoned that I would have to crawl in on my hands and knees. I put my slippers on.

As I made my way to the end of the wall, I still couldn't make out what the odor was but knew this was where it was coming from. I asked my wife to get me a metal coat hanger, so I could move the mound when I saw it. A dead bat lay in the middle of what was now obvious.

"Bat droppings!" I screamed! "We have bats in the attic!"

I couldn't get out of there fast enough. I now had to take a bath. When I went back to bed, I stared at the ceiling while listening to the sounds of bats. "Why, oh, why?" I could now better understand the phrase Winnie-the-Pooh frequently uttered. "Oh bother." Every day since moving to this farm, there seemed to be a new crisis.

The next day, the sun came up, and a new day began. I could think clearly now that the rain was gone. There were so many projects to be done but they would have to wait. I had to get rid of the bats. I frantically started calling hardware stores, feed stores, and whoever else would listen to me. I asked whether they knew anyone who could get rid of bats or whether they had any bat traps or bat poison. Until my last call, everyone I spoke with said no.

Finally, the last hardware store clerk said, "Sure, we have bat traps."

I now felt some relief. I asked, "How do they work?" I had never heard of a bat trap.

He explained, "Well, first, you set the trap, then you lie down on the ground and put it on your jugular vein and wait."

As he was telling me this, I thought about what he was saying and proceeded to question him. "You put it on your jugular vein?" I questioned. I was trying to envision this procedure.

Then he burst out laughing, and I heard him yell, "Harry, I got one, and I got him good!"

Realizing I had been the butt of a practical joke, I hung up. "How could he have no consideration for my dilemma?"

Later in the day, my neighbor Andy, came to visit. I told him what had happened. He too burst out laughing.

"Jawn, you have been took!" he yelled and continued laughing at me, all the while slapping his knee. "He sized ya up as a city slicker!"

And now I was feeling like one.

"Jawn, if you want to get rid of those bats, you gotta get you some sulfur candles."

I asked, "Where do you get them, Andy?"

"Any hardware store should have 'em."

I had never heard of sulfur candles. I asked Andy how they worked. He replied.

"Jawn, I don't know how, but they work. But this is what you gotta do. Seal off the part of the house you're gonna stay in, then you light the candles upstairs and everywhere you ain't a gonna be. Then ya let 'em burn out. When they get a whiff of that sulfur, them bats will leave."

He asked if I knew where they were getting in. I told him I hadn't a clue. After looking around the house, we found a hole up by the roofline in the eaves.

Andy yelled, "That's it! You're gonna have to sit there and wait till they all come out. Then you can plug that hole."

I cried, "Andy, you've got to help me!"

He laughed. "Jawn, what's the matter? Are you afraid of a little old bat?"

I looked him in the eyes and quickly replied, "Yes!"

He laughed again and said. "Oh, all'll right."

He then started to think aloud. "We are gonna need an extra-long ladder, some metal to close it with, a hammer, and some nails." Then he looked at me. I froze, looking at him without saying a word.

"You don't have any of that, do ya, Jawn?"

I looked as helpless as a puppy dog while saying, "No."

"All right, Jawn, you go get the sulfur candles, and I'll get the rest. But we'll have to start when it gets dark"

Later that evening, we sectioned off a portion of the house downstairs and lit the candles upstairs. They were potent. I guessed it was the irritant that made the candles work. We then went outside and waited. By midnight we counted 140 bats flying out of the house and into the moonlit sky. By twelve thirty, we thought they had all left.

Andy said, "Okay, Jawn, go up the ladder and close that hole with this tin."

I looked at the tin, the ladder, and then the hole as one more bat flew out and fell to the ground.

"Andy, would you close that hole?"

"Oh, all'll right, you sissy."

Andy went up the ladder, closed the hole, and came back down. I was so relieved. I knew he could tell by the look on my face that he had just saved my life.

"Jawn, I'm going home to take a shower. I will be back in about an hour to make sure everything is all right."

"Okay, Andy, I will make sure the candles are out, and I'll take a bath" .

After Andy left, I went into the house and got something to drink. I sat down to tell Gloria she wouldn't believe how many bats had been living in the attic. Suddenly we heard chirping and a noise that sounded like the flapping wings of a bird. It was coming from the back of the house in a room off the kitchen.

"No! Could it be?" I looked at Gloria incredulously. Earlier at the bottom of the door between the kitchen and the back room, we had stuffed towels. I pulled back a towel and with a flashlight tried to peek under the large gap at the bottom of the door. As I moved the flashlight to try to get a good look, the chirping grew intense and significantly louder. At this point it had become screeching. I got nervous and quickly put the towel back. I realized bats were now sealed in the back rooms of the lower level of the house.

I asked Gloria to stand behind me with a broom. She asked why. I told her my plan. I would pull back the towel with one hand, and with the hammer in the other hand, I would kill them as they tried to come under the door.

"Why am I holding the broom?" she asked.

I proceeded to explain, "Just in case they come out faster than I can kill them with the hammer, you can be behind me and hit them with the broom and knock 'em to the ground so I can come around and kill them with the hammer." She reluctantly agreed to my plan. We were now ready.

With my left hand, I pulled back the towel and waited. Just as the light peered under the door, they started chirping. Although the sound made me nervous, I kept my cool. Then it happened. A bat wing started coming under the door. I noticed something unusual. In the middle of the bat wing were a couple of fingers feeling their way out from under the door.

We were now both on edge, sleep deprived, exhausted, and truly scared. I was waiting for the head to come out, and I would then execute my plans to hit it with the hammer. The tension was mounting. I raised the hammer, waiting for the opportune moment. Preoccupied with her own fear, Gloria didn't see me raising the hammer to come down on the bat.

I was between her and the bat. As I was about to swing the hammer down, she came down with the broom and hit me on the hand holding the hammer. This, in turn, made me lose control, swing the hammer, hit my thumb, and loudly scream in pain.

She wasn't exactly sure what had happened. She knew she'd hit my hand, but surely I wouldn't scream about being hit by a broom. She wondered whether my scream was the result of the bat biting me. She saw me trying to grab the towel and grabbing my thumb after throwing down the hammer. She finally realized that her broom swing had caused me to hit my thumb. Her next move was to run to the kids, who were fast asleep in the next room.

This fiasco was just too much! I was ready to get d-r-u-n-k— and I mean really drunk.

Andy came back and seated himself in the kitchen. As we reviewed the events of the night, Andy pondered, "How had they gotten into the back rooms of the house?"

We discussed this question for about fifteen minutes. And then I noticed this bright light coming from the direction of the barn, which was around three hundred feet from the house.

The barn had been built into the side of a hill, so the front looked like two stories while the back looked like three. It had a huge silo to the right with a deteriorated roof. The right side of the barn needed a lot of work. As I looked in disbelief there was a roaring fire consuming the barn. It was ablaze.

I panicked. The tractor was near the barn. While running to the tractor, I yelled at Gloria to call the fire department. The heat from the fire was intense.

The week before, the gentleman who had cut my hay put approximately two hundred bales into the barn. This was my share of what he had produced from cutting the fields.

Now the barn, which was ablaze, was consumed into a towering inferno with fresh hay to fuel it. The fire department arrived within fifteen minutes. How that many private vehicles accompanied the fire truck at this hour of the night amazed me.

The first thing they did was wet the house down because of the magnitude of heat coming from the barn. The heat was so hot that it had melted the plastic covering the windows of the old farmhouse. To prevent the house from catching fire, one fire truck continually hosed down the house while the other tried to put out the flames coming from the barn.

We stood there aghast. There was nothing we could do. Finally, the fire seemed to be under control, and the fire chief came to the house with two other men. We went into the parlor and sat down. This room was one of the rooms at the bottom of the stairs that hadn't been sealed off while we were burning sulfur candles. You could still smell the strong odor of sulfur in the room.

The fire chief explained that the fire had burned so fast and intense that there was no saving the barn. He further explained that the hay in the barn looked like it had been freshly cut. I shared with him the events leading up to the hay being there. He finally said, "It looked like it was spontaneous combustion."

I sat back, thought about it, and looked at Andy, who had accompanied me into the parlor. The fire chief said the barn would continue to smolder for days because of the large hand-hewn thick logs that served as the floor system for the barn.

As we sat there, discussing the situation, a bat flew down the stairs. As it flew into the parlor, it fell in the middle of the floor. We all stared at it but didn't move. The fireman looked at it, looked at me (I wasn't moving or making a comment), and then looked back at it, not knowing we had been battling bats all night long. He must have assumed it was a family pet, because none of us moved. We all just sat there and stared at it.

About that time, I softly spoke up. "We have been fighting bats all night." It was now about four thirty in the morning, and I was too exhausted to go into much detail.

Andy calmly walked over, picked up the bat by its wing, and threw it outside.

The fire chief smiled at Andy and said, "I'll be back in the morning to file a report."

I don't quite remember what happened after that, except that I went back to our sealed area and crashed.

The next morning was a new day. I went into the yard and noticed that the maple tree in front of our house was covered with bats hanging from the limbs. I guessed that since they couldn't get back in the house, this was their only place of refuge. The maple tree was covered with bats like Christmas tree ornaments. It seemed that our bat problem was finally over.

I now had no barn, but this loss didn't concern me too much. I hadn't really known what I was going to do with the barn. Remember, I was impressed with the novelty of it, but I wasn't a farmer.

Now a recurring question continued to haunt me. *Why did I ever buy this farm?* The whole next day I reviewed the previous forty-eight hours.

After a couple of days, my breathing returned to normal. I regrouped and returned to fixing up other parts of the house to make it feel like a home.

The following week, the house was beginning to transform into acceptability. It dawned on us that it was time to take a little break. We started making trips to Ligonier. The little Italian restaurant became the family getaway.

We started making friends with the restaurant owner and

the barber next door. And then we met a couple we started to see frequently at the restaurant. During our conversations, we noticed that we had quite a few things in common.

They had also moved from the big city and bought a farm. However, their farm was only three acres and closer to Ligonier. They invited us to their home, which they had been living in for about five years.

Their home was a little different from ours in the sense that it was much older. The foundation was three-foot-thick stone, which really impressed me. As we toured the home, we noticed there was a fireplace in every room.

The kitchen fireplace was enormous, big enough for me to walk in. It had large kettles on long rods with hinges built into the stonework. The rods swung in and out and to and from the hearth to control the amount of flame and heat that came from the fire when cooking.

These fireplaces were breathtaking. Each had been meticulously brought back to its original condition. The gentleman explained that it had been a surprise to him that the fireplaces were even there. When he bought the home, the fireplaces were all covered up with Sheetrock. By accident one was uncovered when they knocked out one of the walls.

At that point he walked outside, looked up, and discovered four flues. They were all in the center of the home. There were four fireplaces. Originally, he had thought the chimneys were for the oil furnace to heat the house. Uncovering the fireplaces was a big surprise to him, and it overjoyed his wife.

We learned that remodeling their home took nearly five years. When he took us to see the basement, he showed us the foundation walls, which were three feet thick at the windows.

You could literally get up in the windowsill and sit. It was absolutely gorgeous.

There was a barn, which was probably half the size of the one we'd had. It had also been brought back to a pristine condition. This wasn't a working farm. The farmland had been sold to a developer, and this was what was left of a working farm from long ago.

This was truly an influential moment for Gloria and me. It encouraged us to return to our farmhouse and try to return it to its pristine condition.

Gloria just knew we had fireplaces all over the house, hidden behind our walls.

I knew she was excited. I tried to calm her down by explaining that the farm we had just seen was at least one hundred years older than ours. By the time I made my second trip back into the house, carrying our groceries, Gloria had already taken a hammer and punched a big hole in one of the walls.

I yelled at her, "What are you doing?"

"I saw the flue outside! I know there's a fireplace in here!"

As she pulled out a large piece of plaster, she uncovered some old brickwork. It didn't look finished and refined like the house we had just left. It was very crude. I finally got her to slow down and stop before she ripped out the whole wall. I went down to the basement, and under where she had been banging on the wall was a huge coal furnace.

I ran back upstairs and stopped her. I told her that what she had uncovered was the back of the chimney for the coal furnace down in the basement.

She then ran to the second floor. On the second floor above the wall she had been working on, there was a square pillar with a flue vent covering where a flue pipe would have gone in.

She now realized that our home was so much "newer" and that previous owners had heated not with a fireplace but with a coal furnace This discovery was a major disappointment to Gloria.

Since I didn't feel like taking on any new projects, I put a big framed picture over the new hole Gloria had created in the dining room and called it a day.

Chapter 5

THE CALM BEFORE THE STORM

B y now Andy was a frequent visitor. He wanted to make sure he wasn't missing out on any adventures taking place at our house.

One day he asked me, "Jawn, what are you gonna do now?"

"Andy, I'm not sure," I replied.

"Well, surely you're gonna do sumthin'."

I then told him about my secret desire to purchase some cows and become a gentleman farmer. He looked at me quizzically and said, "What's that?"

"Well, Andy, I want to get some cows, but I don't want to milk them. I want to get some beef cows so I can put them in the pasture and just watch them grow."

He said, "Are you gonna ride your horses?"

"No, no, no. I can't ride."

"Jawn, you bought this farm with two hundred thirteen acres. You got a tractor and two horses, and you ain't gonna ride your horses? What's wrong with you?"

"Andy, I can't ride," I confessed.

"Jawn, this Saturday we're gonna change that. I'll come over, saddle up a horse, and I'm gonna give you a riding lesson."

"No, that's all right Andy. I don't need to ride a horse."

"Jawn, there ain't nothing to it. I'll see ya Saturday morning."

After he left, I thought, *I might as well.* I told Gloria we might as well go to town and get ready. She said, "Get ready for what?"

"To ride a horse," I said.

"What do you need to get ready to ride a horse?"

"I don't have a cowboy hat, I don't have any cowboy boots, and I don't have one of those fancy belt buckles."

She looked at me in disbelief and said, "You don't need all that to ride a horse."

"I know but I ain't never rode a horse, and I need to get my confidence level up." I started to realize I was beginning to talk like Andy.

She knew I was kidding but went along with the plan anyhow. We went to town. I couldn't just get boots for myself, so I got the whole family fitted with boots. I didn't want the boots to be ostentatious, but I definitely didn't want them to look like work boots. I wanted the refined cowboy look, and I certainly never wanted the dairy farm appearance.

Next was the hat. The girls and I got cowboy hats, and the big silver belt buckle was for me. Gloria wanted no part of the hat or buckle. A new pair of jeans for everyone completed our new fashion wardrobe.

While in town getting outfitted, I met Walter, my unique neighbor. I shared with him my plan to get some cows. Walter didn't have any pasture and asked whether he could go in with me and also buy some cows. I agreed that he could keep them on my property.

He went on to say that he had another friend who would probably also like to get involved with our purchase of cows.

He said he'd speak to his friend about the possibility of a three-way deal.

Saturday arrived, and Andy came for my first riding lesson. I had on my new jeans, cowboy boots, shirt, hat, and cowboy buckle. I was now ready to be taught.

Andy asked, "Jawn, are you ready? You ain't chickening out on me, are ya?"

"I don't know. I hope not."

"Well, let's go get the bridle and the horse."

I had been feeding the horses grain in a bucket to get them to come to me. When they saw me with the bucket, they came running to get fed, not ridden.

While the golden Palomino bent its head into the bucket to get fed, Andy put a rope around its neck. With that, he told me to hold the rope and put the bucket down so he could put the bit in the horse's mouth.

Now, this horse hadn't been ridden in over a year, and it didn't really want that bit in its mouth. Not to be intimidated, Andy grabbed the horse by the neck with one hand and put the bridal over its head with the other. Andy was a big man. If he stood in the doorway, there wasn't much light that could be seen around him. So, when he grabbed that horse to put the halter on, he got the job done. He then handed me the bridle as he picked up the blanket and saddle and put it on the horse. It was now ready to ride.

I was now getting nervous. He looked at me and said, "It's time to get on." He could see I was hesitant and shouted, "Jawn, get on the horse!"

He held the reigns, and I got on and held the saddle horn. He went to hand me the reigns, and I said, "No, no, no. Just walk me a little bit."

He looked at me with disgust and started walking with the reigns in his hand. As I looked toward the house, I could see my family waving with big smiles. I smiled and waved back. "Look at me! I'm riding!"

Andy looked at me while rolling his eyes. He said, "Take these reigns and ride him."

"No, you ride him first, and then I will ride after you do."

"Jawn, you're nothing but a sissy!"

"Andy, you got that right!" I said.

"Jawn, you are supposed to let this horse know who's boss."

"Andy, he knows already he is the boss."

He balked. "Get down!" And I did.

Andy got up on the horse like the Lone Ranger and took off. Well, it became obvious the horse hadn't been ridden in a long while and didn't want to be ridden. It took off faster than Andy intended to go. However, Andy managed to turn it around and come back. Andy tried to slow the horse down, but it wouldn't slow down. He then slung one of his legs over the horse, so his body was totally on only one side of the horse as he was coming back. When it got back to where the other horse and I were, it stopped abruptly.

I said, "Andy, I ain't riding this horse."

"Jawn, he just needs to be broken in again. You just ride him a little bit, and he'll be fine."

"Andy, I ain't riding this horse," I said.

With that he put up the saddle, and I went in the house. I felt now that it was time to get drunk, and it was only nine o'clock in the morning.

The next day I met Walter and his friend. We decided to purchase five cows. I got two, Walter got one, and his friend got two. I had the only pasture, so we agreed that they would all be together on my farm. The next step was to locate five good cows. I called around and asked Andy to check around also.

I saw an ad in the newspaper with cows for sale in Washington, Pennsylvania, which is south of Pittsburgh, although at the time I had no idea where Washington, Pennsylvania, was. All I knew was that some guy was selling cows, and I wanted them. I called the number listed in the paper. A gentleman answered and said, "Hello?"

I asked, "Are you the party that has cows for sale?"

"Yes," he replied.

"I am looking for some beef cows. Five to be exact," I proudly responded.

"What kind do you want?"

"I want the kind you don't milk, the ones with the white faces and red bodies."

"You mean Herford's?"

"I don't know. I just know that I want the kind you don't milk."

With that he said, "I've got five Herford heifers, about eight hundred pounds apiece."

"How much do you want for them?"

"Two hundred dollars each. That will be one thousand dollars."

"Now, these aren't the kind you milk, right?"

I heard him at the other end of the line chuckle and say, "No, these are the kind you raise for beef."

"I want them. Will you deliver?"

"Yes, but I want cash," he said. We then made arrangements for the cows to be delivered by the end of the week. I got the cash ready and waited for the delivery, which was set for Friday around six o'clock in the evening.

This was the day I was to become a gentleman farmer. I called my new neighbor partners and shared the good news. Then I pictured myself sitting on the porch and watching the cattle graze and get bigger and bigger.

Andy came by that night, and I shared my news and excitement with him. He didn't seem to understand just why I was so uptight. As far as he knew, that was just a natural way of life. He then asked whether I wanted to go spotting.

I asked, "What is that?"

Andy growled. "Jawn, you don't know what spotting is? Just how long have you lived in the city?"

"All my life," I replied.

Just about then his brother Bill arrived. "Are we going?" he yelled.

Andy said, "I am just trying to explain to Jawn exactly what spotting is." He turned to me. "Jawn, we drive our trucks up into the fields when it gets dark, and when we see a deer, we point a bright light on 'em, and they stand still and wait for us to shot 'em."

I couldn't believe what Andy had said. "That's against the law. Aren't you afraid of the game wardens?"

Bill laughed and said. "No, they won't bother us."

"Why?" I asked.

Bill smiled as he spit out some chewing tobacco. "'Cause we shoot at 'em."

"They won't come back."

He laughed.

Oh no! Where have I moved to? My very friendly neighbors are beginning to concern me.

Andy could see by the look on my face that it wasn't a night to push the issue, so he dropped the topic. We sat on the porch and just watched the night roll in.

Chapter 6

THE COWS JUMPED OVER THE MOON

Finally, it was Friday. The day arrived. I got a phone call from the man with the cows, who said he was going to be about forty minutes later than the original six o'clock appointment. At about eight thirty, he arrived. I was more than a little disappointed, but he was finally here. By now the sky was pitch black. There was no moon.

The man apologized for being so late and asked me just where I wanted him to unload the cows. I said I had a two-acre pasture just behind the house. He then backed his truck up to the fence opening. Although I had a flashlight, the darkness swallowed up the light. I opened the fence and helped direct him back. The grass was two feet high in this pasture, so I sort of shuffled my feet for sure footing. He backed the truck right up to the fence, pulled a latch, and a ramp fell down and hit the ground.

Nothing came out.

He then started yelling at the cows to get out, but I don't think they understood. He stood on the rails of the trailer and tried to persuade them to leave with the slap of a stick on their backs. It seemed to me that he was being a little cruel, but this was his business, so I didn't say a word.

Then it happened.

I heard a set of hooves on the floorboard of the trailer as they started to walk out. Then there was the distinct sound of something running through the grass. I heard this five times, but only once was I close enough to actually put my flashlight on a cow to get a glimpse of just what was getting out. All I knew was that I saw red. I rationalized five distinct swishes to be five distinct cows.

We walked to the front of the truck, and I counted out $1,000. He thanked me, got in his truck, and quickly left. I made sure the fence was secured and closed. Not being able to see anything, I went to the house and shared the news of the arrival of our new animals with Gloria.

The next morning, I got up bright and early with no alarm clock. Daybreak had just struck. I put on my new cowboy boots, belt buckle, and hat. Running out to check out my personal *Ponderosa*, I was walking out to the pasture, and I know that my chest was sticking out just a little farther. As I got closer to the pasture, something was wrong. There were definitely the white-faced and red-body cows, but there were only four of them. I was puzzled.

Just about then the horses in the next pasture got a good look at their new companions and started to make some loud noises. Then I saw it. One of the cows had gotten into the horse pasture. It was then that the golden Palomino reared up like Silver, the Lone Ranger's horse, and really started to whinny and neigh.

The cow in the horse pasture panicked and ran through the fence back into the pasture where it belonged. A big sigh of relief came over me, but I thought, *He ran through the fence!* I walked over to the fence, thinking that all would be well now. I saw the five cows in a huddle and not moving. The horses wouldn't share their farm with these new intruders without making a ruckus. After all, they'd had the farm to themselves for several years. The Palomino started to do the Lone Ranger thing again, snorting and running back and forth in their own pasture.

The cows started to get nervous. They started to walk very fast to the end of the fence. When they couldn't go any farther, they went back to the fence line where I was standing.

Since they couldn't go any farther, they headed back to where they had been. Only now they were moving a little faster. My heart started to race a little as they started to pick up speed. What was I afraid of? I tried to calm myself, thinking, *They're in a fenced pasture.*

Sure, they are afraid. They weren't used to us yet. *It will be all right*, I thought. *It will be all right.* This thought process and the cows' riding the rail went on for about five minutes, and then it happened. At the far end of the field, I witnessed all five cows as they jumped over the four-and-a-half-foot barb-wire fence and out of my life. My heart felt like it was going to jump out of my chest. What was I supposed to do?

My immediate thought was to go after them, so I started to run after them. *No, no, I can never catch them.* I turned around and started to run for the saddles. *I'll saddle up a horse and chase them. No, no, I can't ride.*

I turned around again to run after the cows, knowing I had to chase them on foot. What would I do if I got to them? I immediately turned around again and ran to the house to get a rope. By the time I got to the house, I was utterly exhausted. By now I was totally out of breath.

Gloria was on the porch, and after listening to what had happened, she said, "I'm going to call Andy."

Within ten minutes Andy arrived and asked, "Jawn, what happened?"

"Andy, you're not going to believe this," I said. "I watched all five cows jump over a four-and-a-half-foot-high fence and run west, away from the road."

"Jawn, Jawn, calm down," he said. "You're too excited. That's not what happened at all. You see, them cows were trained. The owner was around the bend with his truck. He called them cows, and they came to him. He loaded them up and took them away."

I said, "What? Andy, I'm excited, I know, but I know what I saw. They didn't go to the road."

Andy saw how upset I was and said. "Jawn, you've got yourself in a thither. I'll get some men, and we'll go a looking for um. But you'll see I'm right."

About an hour later, Andy came back with four other men. One was Andy's brother Bill, but the others were unfamiliar to me. I thanked them for their willingness to help. Andy asked me again what direction I thought the cows had ran, and we headed there. He instructed us all to look for signs of tracks. I, like the rest of them, held my head down and looked, but I really didn't know what I was supposed to find. Tracks of a cow, I guessed.

Then I heard one of the men yell, "They went this way."

I quickly ran to see what the tracks looked like, but with all the leaves on the ground, I could spot nothing. But I wasn't about to say anything. If they knew what they were doing, I was thankful they were there. We kept walking, and someone kept finding tracks, so we kept walking. It was beginning to rain, but we didn't stop. Then he said he had lost their trail and told us all to spread out and look. I was at the end, about twenty feet from the next guy, but I was looking hard for something unknown to me. About twenty minutes later, I got tired and looked over to where I thought the others were.

I couldn't find anyone. I yelled, and no one answered. *Oh no*, I thought. *I'm lost.*

I started angling to the right. They must be in this area. I kept walking and yelling; by now I was soaked to my bones.

About an hour and a half later, all the men went to my house and called for me. Gloria came out and yelled, "He's not here. I thought he was with you."

Andy explained that they had all gone home to change their wet clothes and get rain gear. Then he said, "Boys, Jawn's lost. Let's go find him."

About a half hour later, I came to this wide opening at the north end of the farm. I looked down from the hill, and there it was, my house. While going through the woods, I had really never left my farm. I got home, and Gloria said with a sigh of relief, "They found you."

I asked, "Who found me?"

She had just finished explaining what had taken place when finally, the men came back from their search. We decided to talk to the adjacent farm owners and alert them of the lost cows.

Two weeks went by, and Walter heard about some cows spotted above one of the farms in the hills. So he packed a lunch and spent a day up in a tree to check things out. Andy and I went to see him around lunchtime, but he hadn't seen them yet. He called me that night and told me the cows had come by at dusk.

Now that he had located them, all we had to do was catch them. I called the Pittsburgh Zoo and asked if they had a tranquilizer dart gun. The response was, "What's that?"

I explained that it was what Marlin Perkins used when he had to capture a wild animal. The man told me I had been watching too much TV. I then explained my dilemma, and he said I sure did have a problem. With that he hung up.

Then I called the vet. After explaining the situation and saying that the cows had become wild, he told me to get some Promazine, an animal sedative. I went to the feed store and got it. The clerk told me to add it to some grain and molasses, or they wouldn't eat it.

We had it all planned. On Friday night we would go to the place where the cows had been sighted and before dusk set up five separate piles, so each would have its own concoction. Then we would wait for them to come.

Andy brought five separate ropes, with which we were to capture the cows, and gave one to each of us. I couldn't help but notice that it was an awfully short rope. Well, I thought, it didn't matter anyway because I was sure someone else who knew what he or she was doing would catch them. We waited behind the bushes.

Sure enough, around eight thirty at night, they came to the open area we had set up for them. Noticing the piles, they all went to one pile and ate it up. Then in unison the five of them went to the next pile and so forth until they had devoured all the piles. We figured we would give them at least an hour for the medication to work. It was now after ten o'clock, so we decided it was time.

Slowly we went in different directions, looking for the cows. After eating, they had moved from the area, but we didn't think they had gone too far. I moved ever so slowly and looked straight ahead. There five pairs of eyeballs were gathered in a circle and looking directly back at me. They weren't moving and were only about five feet from me.

My heart started beating so hard that it felt like it was going to come out of my chest. I couldn't just stand there because I had just filled my britches and was sure they were going to smell me. Ever so slowly, I moved closer and tried to put this five-foot rope over one of the cows' heads. When I got within a foot of the cows, they took off. Hearing the noise, everyone ran to where I was, but no one could figure why the cows were so alert and had moved so fast.

The next day I called the vet and told him the drug had no effect on them. He asked me how long we had waited after feeding the cows. I told him over an hour. He explained that a cow has four stomachs, so it takes much longer for medication to take effect.

Because of the molasses and food, these cows started coming back to this area. The farmer closest to the area agreed that we could use one of his fenced areas to capture the cows. We now had a new plan. It was to have the men to go above the area and drive the cows down to the penned area, which we would open for the cows to enter.

I had no Idea what was about to happen, but I was ever so thankful that I had help in trying to retrieve these cows. We went around the hill and started to come down to meet at the place where the cows were supposed to be. We finally arrived to meet them where they were resting.

As we approached them, they got up and started down the

hill toward the trap we had set for them. Three of the cows, however, went in the opposite direction, but two proceeded toward our trap. It was now or never.

We got around them and tried to coax them into the corral. One went in, but the other took off. No matter—at least we had one. I was elated.

Andy now said, "Boys, we have to get this one to Jawn's farm." He shared with us how we were going to do this. We would lay long ropes with a lasso at one end on the ground and wait for the cow to walk onto it; then we would catch it by the leg. We were doing well—we had a plan.

I'm sure we were a sight—four guys holding one eight-hundred-pound cow by one foot. Andy then threw a rope over the horns and then another. He split us into two groups, one on each side of the cow and told us to pull it toward the road. Four of us couldn't budge that cow.

Andy said, "Boys, hold on tight cause she is going to move now." Without explaining what was to happen next, Andy got behind the cow and wound its tail into a corkscrew. He took a deep breath and said, "Boys, she is going to move. Be ready."

We stood there and gripped the rope a little tighter. We expected the cow to start walking.

Andy took one last twist of her tail, and that cow jumped at least five feet in the air. The reaction frightened all of us on the ropes, and we all jumped back and fell to the ground almost at once. We got up as fast as we could and picked up the rope we had just dropped.

Thankfully, when the cow landed, she didn't move. She just stood there. Andy yelled, "All right, boys. Let's do this again." We continued this process for about one hundred yards, then gradually got the cow onto a trailer. We got it home and put it in a small fenced area we had prepared for just this occasion.

Two weeks later we heard that the cows had moved to an adjacent hill, not far from the first. Again ropes were planted on the ground, and someone waited for the appropriate time to capture one by the foot again and tie it to a tree. Andy got his brother to bring his dad's tractor, and this time, with the rope around the horns again, he would pull this cow to the trailer in the clearing.

Andy had the situation under control, I thought. But when he pulled the cow by the horns, her head went down, and she held all her hooves as stiff as a board. She made this loud moo, and I saw her tongue sticking our as she started to dig four furrows. Her head looked like it was about to be pulled off.

Concerned, I said to Andy, "Do you think she is all right?'

To which a disgusted Andy replied, "Shut up, Jawn." Without another word, Andy got the cow into the fenced area and went home.

By now two months had passed, and the other cows had become wild, and I couldn't get close to them. The other two who had purchased the cows with me were so frustrated by this time that they just went out and shot the cows. They gave most of the beef to the people who had helped. About twenty-four hundred pounds of beef went a long way.

By now the captured cows had become pets. The molasses mixed with the grain I fed them helped me become their best buddy.

Chapter 7

TALKING TREES

After three months, almost everything involved in living on the farm had settled down. The two captured cows felt like this was home and would run to me anytime I went near them with grain. The horses had finally accepted their new neighbors. Andy stopped coming around as much as he previously had. I think he was afraid that he might get involved in another fiasco or that I might ask him to help.

Then it happened. One day my oldest daughter, Kelly, was coming down the stairs and tripped on her oversized nightgown; she fell all the way to the bottom. I ran and picked her up in my arms, just fast enough to see her eyes close and slide into unconsciousness. I was scared to death.

Gloria quickly called my father (who was a physician in Florida) and gave me the phone. I then asked what to do. He replied, "Get her to the hospital, you stupid idiot." I did feel stupid.

We all got in the car and rushed her to the hospital. I felt so guilty. Why had we ever moved? Every possible question was now tormenting me. Her fall was now my fault. I was judge and jury. I didn't deserve this child God had given me.

The emergency room doctor felt Kelly had a concussion. But they wouldn't know the extent of the trauma for at least twenty-four hours. I got a motel room, about a half a mile away in Latrobe, for Gloria and Kerry; and went back to the hospital to stay with Kelly. It was one of the most agonizing nights I think I've ever had.

The next morning, she was wide awake and talking like everything was fine. After the doctor examined her, he confirmed that Kelly was going to be all right. We went home, and I had a new prospective on my family. This had truly been a life-changing event. I thanked God over and over for my family, especially my girls.

In the city of Johnstown, Pennsylvania, which wasn't that far away, I heard something about a major flood that had taken place years before. I read up on this tragedy and decided to see this town, which had a dam that kept it from being flooded again. I knew my children were too young to appreciate the history, but it would be a family outing.

When we got there, I noticed some historical marks on some buildings, indicating the levels of the flood. It had risen to the second story of most of the downtown area. The realization that so many had died in the flood and the fact that flooding had happened more than once now had a devastating effect on me.

On the way home, we stopped by a farm with long ears of corn still on the stalks. Gloria asked me to stop; she wanted to quickly gather some. I told her that would be stealing. She reassured me that she would take only enough for a meal for the family and that the farmer would never miss it.

We got home, and the excitement of picking her own corn right off the stalk consumed her. She immediately shucked it and began boiling it. When she was done, she was surprised to see that each ear had many colors. She quickly put it on the table, and we sat down to eat it. It looked like corn; it felt like corn, but it wasn't sweet. As a matter of fact, it didn't taste good, so we set it aside.

Later that day, Andy came by, and we sat in the kitchen. He saw the cooked corn and asked why we were cooking field corn. With a grin, he let me know this was the corn fed to cows. He laughed and asked, "How did it taste?" I gave no answer but felt like a real sucker.

My family and Gloria's immediate family lived in Florida, but no one had come to visit. Gloria's aunt, who lived in Jeannette, Pennsylvania, came to visit once, but after seeing just how far from civilization we were, she never came again. My Uncle John and Aunt Judy were motor home buffs and would travel the United States on a whim. However, Uncle John was a very secretive man and would never let me know his intentions.

So unannounced, he came, and what a delight—a family member had come to visit. He fell in love with the farm and said I could have free hydroelectricity. He went on to explain that the force of the water coming off the mountain could create the needed energy to generate electricity. With all that had already taken place, he scared me with the thought of getting into something else I knew nothing about.

My brother Joe was going to Boston University at the time and said he would like to visit and bring a family friend, Danny, to visit. I got excited again. You see, with the farm life settling down, it became just so peaceful and unnerving that it was starting to get to me. I enjoyed my family more than ever, but this change in lifestyle, from always being on the go to "Let's just sit around and watch the rust grow on the bumper of the car," was just too much.

Joe arrived two days before Thanksgiving. He said he wanted to cook the Thanksgiving Day turkey. Gloria got excited. A big smile came over her face when she realized she wouldn't have to do it. The next thing he said was that both he and Danny wanted to go to the hot spot in town to party. To quote him, they were "going to look for two-legged deer." After all, it was a school break, and surely there was a party somewhere. He, like I, had a hard time visualizing just how far from city life we had moved.

I told him about a ski resort, called Seven Springs, about an hour away. That was fine by him. If there was a party, he wanted to be there. So that night they left for Seven Springs Ski Resort.

About twenty minutes later, they were back in the house, horrified and talking a mile a minute.

"Slow down," I said. "Only one of you talk at a time."

"We hit a deer," they yelled in unison.

Joe said, "It just jumped out in front of us. We couldn't avoid hitting it."

I asked whether it had run away.

"No," they said, "it's still in the middle of the road."

I picked up my rifle and told them to get in my Jeep. We went to where it lay and put it into the back of the Jeep. I told them to hurry because it wasn't deer season, and we could get in trouble. When we got home, a big sigh of relief came over the two of them. They had thought for sure they were going to jail, but now were safe.

They even got a little excited. Neither had gone hunting before, and now they had gotten their first deer. They wanted to know just what to do next. I told them we had to gut it and hang it.

"So who is going to gut it?" I asked.

They just looked at each other, and Danny said, "We don't know how. Would you?"

I knew I really didn't have a choice. I had gotten pretty good at it. I had lost a coin toss on shooting my first deer and had to do it myself. It stank; it was messy, but if you kill it, you have to clean it.

They never went looking for a party again while visiting me. I think they were afraid of hitting another deer. Joe started to organize everything he needed to make the big meal for Thanksgiving. I took him to our little town of Bolivar to get what groceries we didn't have on hand.

Joe then announced that it would take twenty-four hours to cook his turkey. I asked, "Why so long?" He said that his recipe took twenty-four hours at 170 degrees. I questioned the temperature. But he let me know he knew what he was doing and that I shouldn't worry about it. He later divulged that really this was an experiment. When the bird came out, it was still raw.

Joe said, "Dang, what's wrong with your range?' I informed him that the range was only three months old. Gloria cut the turkey into slices, pan-fried them, and saved the meal.

When Joe and Danny arrived, there was snow on the ground, and my sister-in-law Marty had just arrived for a visit the day before. Although there was snow on the ground, Marty wanted to ride the black-and-white horse. I agreed but said she would have to saddle it.

"No," she said, "I'd rather ride bareback with a bit in its mouth."

I showed her where the bits were, and off she went out into the snow-covered pasture. She looked like she was having a good old time.

Kerry, my youngest, asked, "Where is Aunt Marty?"

I looked back as if to say *Right there*, but Marty was nowhere to be seen, and the horse was going in the opposite direction with no one on his back. The sight sure was a puzzle. I kept looking and started to yell for Marty. Then I saw her head pop up out of the snow with a big smile on her face. She yelled, "Here I am!"

She had fallen into a snow drift and was totally out of sight. We all laughed at the sight, but I had to give her credit for even getting on the horse.

The next day Joe and Danny wanted to help and realizing there wasn't a winter shelter for the animals, they volunteered to build a lean-to for them. They had fun scavenging around the farm and looking for materials to build in this protected area. Then they put it in a cart and pulled it with the tractor to an area we had agreed to for building this shed. They both did this without help from me. I was truly impressed.

The shed proved to be a lifesaver as the cold winter progressed. One day my brother Joe asked me whether he could go fishing in the pond. I said, "Sure, but it might be frozen." He didn't seem too concerned, so I thought nothing of it. Later in the day, I went down to the pond to see how he was doing. When I got there, I was surprised to see him fishing on top of the ice. I asked him why he didn't cut a hole in the ice to fish. He responded that if he caught a fish, he would have to clean it, and it was just too cold to do that. I couldn't help but wonder whether we came from the same gene pool.

A few weeks later my cousins from Georgia called and said they'd heard about the large deer population in our area. They asked if they could come to hunt. Wow! This was getting exciting; more people were coming to visit. John and Frank were quite a few years older than I, so I felt honored that they wanted to visit, even if it was only for hunting. They were avid hunters, and part of their pilgrimage in hunting was to go to the nearest pub after a good day of hunting and just get wasted. I explained how to get to Annie Potts's place, and they left.

When they got there, they saw a pickup truck parked in front of the place with the biggest deer they had ever seen lying in its bed. They walked closer to get a better look and then went inside. At the bar there was a hunter bragging about how he had won the deer pool that was going on. He went on to say that they should just give him the money now. The commotion was getting hot because there were still three days left for the contest. After he told them the deer was on his truck, a couple of guys ran out to see it.

Someone then yelled out, "Where is this big buck that's making you so proud?"

"Out in the bed of my truck!" he said with a big grin. A couple more men went out with the hunter to see this prize trophy, but when they got there, the truck was empty. The hunter became unglued.

"Someone stole my deer!" he yelled.

Then a clear voice spoke up. "Sure, they did. Nice joke."

My cousins later explained that there was no way they were going to get involved with this "scene from *Deliverance*."

We lived on venison the whole time we lived on the farm. It wasn't uncommon to go to the basement and find one hanging to cure. I became very proficient at cutting and cooking venison. It wasn't a delicacy in our house but a staple. After hunting season everyone left. It took time, but I finally got a handle on how to work the coal furnace.

Something came up in Florida regarding the tenants in

a house we owned and rented. Gloria volunteered to go and straighten it out. I wanted to go, but someone had to care for the animals. Her father said he would come to Pennsylvania during this time. He wanted to see this farm-style living we kept talking about, and while here, he wanted to see some of his friends in the Jeanette, Pennsylvania, area.

One day he wanted to go to Annie Potts place and get a six-pack of beer. On the way he saw a Hells Angels biker coming from the other direction; for whatever reason, he decided to shoot him a bird. He must have felt safe since they were going fast enough in opposite directions. He got to Annie Potts and got out of the car just in time to see this motorcycle speeding in his direction. He recognized the motorcycle driver as the one he'd just flipped out.

He nonchalantly started to walk toward the bar door as the biker yelled, "Hey you stop there!" He got off his bike.

My father-in-law, with his heart beating a mile a minute, put a smile on his face and replied, "Howdy, neighbor. Can I help you?"

"You just flipped me off back there."

"No, I didn't flip you off. I was waving with a howdy-neighbor wave." He stuck two fingers together and made a similar gesture but in a different direction with a smile on his face.

"No, you didn't. You flipped me off."

My father-in law started to sweat and again repeated himself, showing the new gesture. "Why? I don't even know you. Why would I flip you off? I was just trying to be neighborly. I'm just visiting."

Ralph must have been convincing because he said the biker gave him a dirty look, got back on his bike, and rode off. As Ralph told me this story, he laughed intensely, feeling that he had outwitted this biker. "You coward. You didn't even stand up for your actions," I chided. "John, what did you expect me to do? After all, my bursitis is acting up. I couldn't have defended myself. He would have made mincemeat out of me." "You had no business flipping him off in the first place just because he rides a bike," I said. "Yeah, well, all right, but I still think it's funny." Finally, my father-in-law went home when Gloria and the kids came back from Florida.

I felt a little alienated from the town and never really fit in. It seemed unusual to the town that at my young age I was able to purchase this well thought of farm, yet not have to work for a living. Flashing one hundred-dollar bills in town and being of Italian heritage led the people to surmise that I must be Mafia.

Day after day, I would walk those beautiful pastures, come home, and relax. Life, however, was getting dull. One day while walking, I started talking to the trees. By the end of the month, I started to hear them talk back. I shared this event with Gloria, and we both knew it was time. We started to make plans to sell the farm and move back to Florida. Our perspective on life had changed, and we felt we had come a long way in our appreciation.

I asked Gloria whether she wanted to take a farewell walk around the farm. Thinking this was a good idea, we both walked up the hill toward the tree line. The magical beauty of the farm was now showing up more than ever. Gloria migrated toward the center of the field, and I went toward the tree line at the fence. I peered out into the woods and just stood still.

As my eyes adjusted to the surroundings, I saw the biggest buck of my life staring back at me. He hadn't moved, but I guess he felt threatened, because he snorted and started scratching the ground with his hooves. I had seen this action before on TV when the matador was about to wave a red cape for the bull to charge. I had nothing to protect myself, and I could now see he had his family behind him. I slowly started to walk backward.

Gloria saw my unusual behavior and yelled out, "What's the matter?"

I softly said, "We have to get out of here now."

I'm not sure whether she could detect my shaking or smell my britches, but she started to run home. Her running in itself scared me further, and I started to also run. The deer then ran off in the other direction.

This event brought us back to reality—we didn't belong here.

We advertised to sell the farm and got a few calls, but when we described that someone had to get lost to find us, most didn't peruse the opportunity. One man thought it would be a good investment and was going to come when a young couple from a town about thirty-five minutes away came and fell in love with it. I shared that at dusk between thirty to forty deer come down to graze in the fields, and that was it—he was sold. He had to come back and witness this event for himself.

A few days later, he came with his brother-in-law, and we drove into the fields to see this sight. Gloria wanted to come, so the three of them rode in the truck, and I volunteered to ride in the back bed. I told him to drive slowly as I braced myself while standing and leaning on the roof with my rifle. I don't know what we were thinking. Driving through the fields and making all that ruckus were no ways to sight a deer. However, I hadn't shown any smarts up to this point, so how was I supposed to show them now?

He drove from one pasture to another as if we were on a safari, and while not paying attention, his tire hit a small ditch, and we came to an abrupt stop. My body, not being secure, didn't stop, and I flew over the top of the truck. I did a 360-degree cartwheel in the air and landed about fifteen feet in front of the stopped truck. My rifle had landed just before me, and I realized I could have killed myself.

I was still trying to get up when they got out of the truck to help me. The man's young brother-in-law thought my flight had been awesome and wanted to know how I did it. Gloria laughed immediately, knowing that in no way had I done it on purpose.

We sold the farm and moved back to Florida with no regrets.

Chapter 8

WE'RE OUTTA HERE

A sigh of relief came over us when we decided to return to Florida and the city life we were accustomed to. We were fish out of water without question. With this decision came the challenge of selling the farm, which was out in the middle of nowhere, within a reasonable amount of time. Quickly we started advertising our nemesis.

We couldn't believe how quickly we were able to sell the farm. I guessed there were other people looking for a change as well. Making a 25 percent profit made me feel like I hadn't lost my touch. Of course, this fact went to my head. However, we had to take an A-frame house in a ski resort area as a trade for the transaction to take place. My desire to get back to civilization was so great that I would have to deal with this additional house later.

So again, we rented the biggest Ryder truck and U-Haul trailer, and we began the long trip back to Florida. This would have been the end of my story if not for a very dear friend Jim. He has a Christian radio program and asked why I didn't include what happened when we got back to Florida.

You can imagine by now that I was coming back with a very

different perspective on what was important in life. Before the farm, life had been all about making money and being successful for my family. Now my family relationship became more important than financial independence and success. My family was now more precious. Watching my children grow with a desire to direct and be involved became more important than just having them be nice to come home to after a hard day.

When we moved to the farm, we kept a rental house in Florida. Our renter left and destroyed our house with two dogs that weren't supposed to be present on the property. We had to get the house restored before we got back, but at least we had a place to come back to. The house was move-in ready when we arrived, which was a relief. We quickly unpacked and got settled.

My days of leisure had come to an end, and to be honest, I was happy and ready to get busy. After searching for a job for more than three weeks with no prospects in sight, I became a little depressed. I found an ad in the paper that talked about the city of Treasure Island creating jobs for people who wanted to work during the recession that was taking place. The job description was to sweep the streets and beautify the city. I was now property rich and cash poor, and eager to work. I found myself in a room with about twelve applicants filling out a questionnaire.

After filling out my application, a man in charge came over to me and said, "You put down that you were a research chemist. Why do you want to sweep the streets?"

I said, "I have a family to feed. I'll do anything."

He went on to explain that they needed a lab tech and that if I wanted to work in the lab, the work would be easier than sweeping the streets, and I was surely overqualified.

I replied, "Sure."

He remarked that he was glad, and he wanted to show me around the lab so I could see the operation. I thought, *all right, I'm getting some specialized attention.* I never thought about why they would have a laboratory, but then I heard the words *Sanitation Department.* As he was describing my duties, he slipped in the word's *sewage treatment.* Right then I panicked. A hot flash came over me, and I became too embarrassed to tell this man I couldn't do it. I couldn't even change my daughter's diapers.

One day Gloria had been at her mother's house, and my youngest daughter, Kerry, had dumped one smelly load in her diaper. *Oh no*, I thought. *What am I going to do?* Gloria was nowhere in sight, and Kerry started to cry. She didn't like the situation any more than I did. I had no choice, I had to change her diaper. In my mind I thought, *Be the man. You can do it.*

I put her on the bed and grabbed a new diaper. As I removed the safety pins and opened the diaper, the heinous smell overtook me, and I began to gag. "I can't do this," I yelled as I quickly put the pins back in and ran to another room to breathe.

In desperation I got a clothespin to pinch my nose and tried again. Emotions were running high, and I was gagging all over the place. I unpinned the diaper once again, and as I was about to remove the diaper, the phone rang. I don't know what possessed me to think the phone had to be answered at that moment, but I did. I quickly repinned the diaper and ran to the phone down the hall.

With the clothespin still on my nose, I answered the phone. It was Gloria. As soon as I recognized her voice, I blurted out, "I can't talk now" and hung up the phone.

As I ran back down the hall to Kerry, still on the bed, I

thought, *My voice sounded a little funny on the phone. Oh well. I've got to get this over with.* I started to unpin the diaper again, and again the phone rang. This fetish of answering the phone got the best of me again, and so again I repinned the diaper and ran to the phone.

It was Gloria again. I lost it. *I am fighting the battle of my life, and she wants to talk*, I thought. In a defiant voice, I said, "I told you I can't talk now" and hung up.

Not realizing that I was creating tension on the other end of the phone line, I ran back to Kerry. I pulled off her diaper and threw it in the bathtub. As I cleaned her off and put her new, clean diaper on, the phone rang.

This time I wasn't stopping for anything. I had to get this over with. I was so emotional that I didn't want to talk to anyone. After I thought Kerry was set and ready to play again, I shut the bathroom door and finally picked up the phone, which had been ringing the whole time. At the other end of the phone, Gloria screamed, *"Don't hang up. What is the matter?"*

By now my breathing was slowing down; the crisis was over. I calmly replied, "I was changing Kerry's diaper." "What?" she screamed. "You had me panicking over you changing a diaper." I said, "Sorry, but you know I can't handle a loaded diaper full of organic noxious fumes."

Now I just knew I couldn't do this job, but the superintendent kept talking, so I really couldn't explain anything right then. I followed him up the side of this large tank, about fifteen feet in the air, with a walkway all around. As we were walking, he kept explaining the operation, but I noticed something strange. When I looked down into this black churning liquid, there was no odor. I then asked why it didn't stink. He replied that it was because of aerobic bacteria. He went on to explain that aerobic bacteria break down the organic material when oxygen is introduced, and there is no odor. He went on to explain that closed systems (septic tanks) work just the opposite and give off gaseous odors.

Wow, I thought. *Maybe I can do this. It's not poop. Its organic material, and it doesn't stink.*

So, he never heard my concerns, and I took the job. The job turned out to be a piece of cake. I was able to do all my sampling and testing in sixty minutes in the morning and then again for sixty minutes in the afternoon. *Unbelievable,* I thought.

As I became comfortable with the job, I became relaxed and got to know the other workers, an unusual bunch of characters. After I was introduced, one of the men asked another where his teeth were. He replied that they were in his mouth. He looked at me and explained that about six months ago, while he was pulling up the aerobic lines from the bottom of the vat to clean them, his teeth had fallen out of his shirt pocket and into the large vat. He went on to explain that about one week ago, he was pulling up the aerobic line again, and he couldn't believe his eyes when he spotted his teeth caught on one of the spray heads he was going to clean. With that he opened his mouth with a big smile and proudly showed me his newfound false teeth. He said, "See?"

I almost barfed right there and had to be excused.

The superintendent and I became good friends. He was very impressed with how quickly I got the job done. One day as he stopped by my lab, he asked me, "Have you ever read the Bible?"

I replied, "No."

To which he responded, "Why?"

I said, "The Bible was written by man. It's just another book."

With unbelievable wisdom he asked, "How much is one plus one?"

"Two," I replied.

"How much is two plus two?"

"Four," I said.

He again pursued me with "How much is four plus four?"

I said, "Where are you going with this?"

He then asked again, "How much is four plus four?"

I said, "Eight"

He asked, "Why?"

I stopped for a moment and thought. Math had been my minor in college, and I was very good at it. I thought that if I had been taught that one plus one equaled the numerical number three, I would have died defending it. Yet I had never read this Bible, and here I was, commenting on it. I responded, "Good one."

He then asked me, "If I brought you a book to read, would you read it?"

"Sure," I said. "With so much time on my hands, it would help pass the time away."

The next day he brought in a book called *The Late, Great Planet Earth* by Hal Lindsey. "Thank you," I replied.

After he left, I began to read it. The first few chapters were about historical background, which at that time of my life didn't interest me but were needful to demonstrate the significance of prophecy. The book finally got very interesting to the point that I couldn't put it down. Then I came to an ultimatum in the book, where I was challenged to know God. Mr. Lindsey quoted scripture and said, "Behold I stand at the door [of your heart] and knock; if anyone hears my voice and opens the door, I will come in to him and dine with him, and he with me." (Revelation

3:20 NKJV). I thought for a moment and pondered that if there is a God, I must know it! He then went on to explain that I could open the door by inviting Jesus Christ into my life. At that moment I did just that. I said I was a sinner and that I was trusting in him to go to heaven. But after I said my prayer, I went on to read the book.

However, this was a big moment. I had grown up with a mother who always made sure I went to church with her. My father was more passive in this area, but as time grew on, he also attended church with Mom and the family. At a very young age, I sang in the choir until my voice changed. I never really understood that this God in heaven was looking down on us and watching what we were going to do.

When it came time for college, I went to the University of Miami. I was in a college apartment with four bedrooms, and each bedroom contained two beds. I was thrown into a very diverse group of eight from all over the world.

One Friday night students from other units came to our downstairs apartment and brought tons of beer. It didn't take very long for all of us to become very friendly. We were getting loose—talking, laughing, and having a great time. Then out of nowhere one of the guys yelled out, "Is there a God?"

Everyone just stopped in thought, and the room became silent. Someone else said, "Yeah, sure, there is a God!"

The questioner said, "Prove it."

This was turning into very a deep conversation. As I looked around the room, it became obvious that there were many different religions represented there. There was a professed atheist, an agnostic, a couple of Baptists, a couple of Catholics, a Hindu, and a Jewish student. Also, there were several who had never revealed just what their religious beliefs were. You can just imagine these students with diverse backgrounds from all over the world openly disusing their religious beliefs. No one was trying to convert anyone; it was just an honest discussion. Although I wasn't practicing my religion it seemed my convictions had to be correct and theirs wrong. Listening to their testimonies and fervent devout positions it caused my mind to ponder. If I had been born into any of these other religions would I be thinking like them? Was I just a product of my environment and traditions?

When I left college, I got married, never to practice any religion. Now I was confronted with that same unanswered question. Is there a God? And do I want to know? Yes, I need to know if there is a God.

"God," I said, "if you are real, I want to know you. I want you to come into my heart and save my soul. I'm trusting in your Son, Jesus Christ. I want to be what you want me to be."

As I kept reading the book about prophecies fulfilled and prophecies to come, I became intrigued. *Why haven't I heard of these things?* I thought. I was now on a quest, and I had to know the truth. I had to find out and do whatever it took to know the truth. My desire to read this Bible and whatever I could get my hands on to find out became my focus. I wasn't going to take anyone's word for it.

During this time my brother-in-law had just come home from Japan with his new Japanese wife. While he was eating at a McDonald's, a missionary couple from Japan, Del and Marilyn, noticed his wife's heritage and started to converse with her in Japanese. They became instant friends. The missionary couple had just arrived from Japan, and the husband and wife were now also socially deprived. The missionary couple invited them to church, and their friendship grew. Their relationship wasn't only Christ centered, but their desire to help me in my journey became their next plan.

I had learned to play tennis in college, and although I wasn't a good athlete, I loved the sport. Knowing this, my brother-in-law set up a tennis date and invited his new missionary friend, Del. We played with great vigor and enjoyed just relaxing and talking at the end. They knew I didn't have a relationship with God and wanted to make sure I had an opportunity to find out. This happened just before I read *The Late, Great Planet Earth*, and I was hesitant to talk about this touchy subject. I didn't want anyone pushing his or her religion or God on me.

We kept playing tennis, and I was now reading for myself to find out about God. My wall of separation started to fall, and I was asking questions, for which they seemed to have answers. I kept listening and reading on my own. While in college, I read all the time; but after graduation I kept too busy to even pick up a book. While on the farm, I'd had all the time in the world to read but no desire. Now I couldn't quench this insatiable desire to find out about this God. The words "Is there a God? Prove it" kept reverberating in my mind.

When I prayed to God, no earth-shaking experience took place, but for the next three days, I was happy as a lark. It seemed like I was walking three feet higher than the walkway. I grew in my understanding of God as I read the Bible many times. I also read books corroborating the Bible that weren't part of the Bible. Then I discovered the most compelling argument that Jesus Christ was God in the flesh by just reading and hearing how the apostles acted.

They all left their jobs and walked with Jesus, listened to him, and watched him preform many miracles. They were convinced that he was The Messiah. But after Jesus's death, they were devastated and felt it was all over. They didn't know what to do and basically fell apart. When they were all together except Thomas, Christ appeared to them alive. They couldn't believe their eyes.

They told Thomas, but he didn't believe them. Again, Christ appeared to the apostles, but this time Thomas was there. In disbelief, Thomas confirmed the Spirit of God in Christ by physically touching his wounds. Christ said, "Thomas, because you have seen Me, you have believed. Blessed are those who have not seen and yet have believed." (John 20:29 NKJV)

But now there was a transformation. Christ had risen from the dead. He was alive. They now knew that he had to be The Messiah. So they went out and preached about Christ being The Messiah without fear of losing their lives. Now they were convinced. This is confirmed according to references outside the Bible that they were convicted by putting their lives on the line to preach Christ as The Messiah. The warnings received (to stop preaching Christ as the messiah) now meant nothing, for they were convinced of the coming life after death. Christ was alive, and they'd witnessed him. They were now ready to preach the gospel and die for it, if necessary. Most of the apostles died a martyr's death. They tried to kill John but he didn't die, so they sent him to a lifetime of prison on the Isle of Patmos.

In a court of law, I believe this evidence would be enough for a conviction of proof. I hope I've encouraged you enough to search for this very important revelation for yourself. Don't take anyone's word for it; find out for yourself. I believe we will be accountable for our actions one day. What will you say you did to find out whether there is a God?

Most people feel that they are truly good. We measure our morality by those around us, but we all have different standards we use. However, if we use God's standard would we feel the same? Ask yourself the following questions and answer them truthfully.

#1) Have you ever lied to anyone for any reason? I believe if you are truthful you would say, YES.

#2) Have you ever stolen anything no mater how small? YES.

#3) Have you ever looked at anyone with lust? Again, if truthful, you would say, YES.

"But I say to you that whoever looks at a woman to lust for her *has already committed adultery with her in his heart"* *(NKJV). Mathew 5:28*

By your own admission you are a lying, thieving, adulterer and these are only three of the commandments. In Romans 3:23 it says

"For all have sinned and fall short of the glory of God". *(NKJV) Romans 3:23*

A) If you want to know if Jesus is real:

1) Ask Jesus to come into your heart and save your Soul.
2) Repent from your past sins.
3) Surrender your life to Christ.
4) Trust in Jesus paying for your sin debt on the cross.
5) Ask God to make himself real in your life.

It's as easy as that if you truly mean it.

An Example of your prayer might be:

Jesus, I'm trusting in you to save me. Please forgive me for my past sins. I believe you died on the cross for me and I want you as my savior and Lord. I surrender myself to you and want to live the rest of my life for you.

In your own words but essentially letting Jesus know that you have surrendered and are trusting in him for everything.

B) If you have interest in learning more about The Messiah, please go to: www.YouGotOurTract.com

C) If you have questions Please go to www.RZIM.org. There are podcasts, look for the ones which address your concerns, in addition to other resources which should help in your journey.

D) If you like videos, please go to www.YouTube.com and view "Ravi Zacharias debate" ... also view "Ray Comfort debate".

About the Author

After Graduating from the University Of South Florida and entering the sciences world as a Chemist John was faced with a major turning point in his life. American Cyanamid, his employer, faced with government resolve to update its Florida Chemical plant or shut it down decided to layoff this Chemical Plant location. NASA also had a very large layoff and it became very hard to stay in the science world. Redirecting his efforts to Pharmaceutical Sales became monumental in having him realize he was a people person and cloistered lab life would never again enter his radar. Enjoying sales and investing became his new efforts, earning him enough money to undertake this unbelievable adventure as portrayed in this book.

Printed in the United States
By Bookmasters